# Spirit Animal List And Their Meanings

Heather .R Peacock

# Introduction

This is a comprehensive exploration into the profound world of shamanism, offering readers a valuable resource for understanding and connecting with animal spirit guides. The guide opens with a quick yet insightful overview of shamanism, providing a foundational understanding of this ancient practice that has been an integral part of various cultures across the globe.

The concept of shamanism is introduced in a way that invites readers to comprehend its diverse manifestations. The guide delineates the different types of shamanism, emphasizing their unique characteristics and applications. Whether exploring core shamanism or delving into specific cultural practices, readers are guided through the essential beliefs and rituals that define shamanic traditions.

One of the key elements explored is the Tree of Life, a symbolic representation that transcends cultural boundaries. The guide takes readers through the significance of the Tree of Life in shamanic cosmology, illustrating its role as a conduit between different spiritual realms. This foundational knowledge sets the stage for understanding the interconnectedness of the shamanic worlds and the intricate paths shamans navigate during their journeys.

Distinguishing between animal spirit guides, power animals, and totems is a crucial aspect of the guide. It clarifies the nuanced roles these entities play in shamanic practices, dispelling common misconceptions. This section serves as a valuable guide for readers seeking a deeper understanding of the spiritual allies that can accompany them on their shamanic journey.

The practical aspects of connecting with animal spirit guides are thoroughly addressed. Through visualization meditation and shamanic journeying, readers are offered step-by-step guidance on how to initiate contact with their power animals. The guide underscores the importance of this connection, highlighting the wisdom and guidance that animal spirit guides can impart to individuals.

An intriguing aspect of the guide is the exploration of power animal magic, tools, and crafts. Rituals involving animal parts are discussed, shedding light on the ethical considerations and the spiritual significance of such practices. The guide presents a holistic perspective on working with power animals, encompassing healing techniques and rituals that readers can incorporate into their own shamanic practices.

The section on animal medicine unveils the profound role of animals in shamanic cultures as healers and conduits of spiritual energy. Readers gain insights into how animal medicine operates and its potential impact on healing. The guide provides practical techniques for connecting with power animals for healing purposes, offering a repertoire of methods that align with diverse spiritual practices.

To enrich the reader's journey, the guide concludes with an extensive list of animal spirit guides and their meanings. This serves as a valuable reference, allowing individuals to deepen their understanding of the symbolic significance and spiritual attributes associated with various animals.

In essence, this book as an indispensable guide for those navigating the intricate realms of shamanism. It seamlessly blends theoretical knowledge with practical insights, providing a holistic approach to understanding, connecting with, and honoring animal spirit guides in the profound tapestry of shamanic exploration.

# Contents

# PART ONE: Animal Spirit Guides in Shamanism

# Chapter 1: A Quick Shamanic Guide

In this section, you'll learn all about the Animal Spirit Guides you'll be working with as you explore Shamanism. However, before you can discover your spirit guides, you'll first need to understand Shamanism and what these guides actually are.

## Understanding Shamanism

Shamanism is a religion that traces its roots to indigenous and tribal societies across Northern Europe, Northern Asia, and the Americas. The word "shamanism" is likely a derivation of the Tungusic word šaman ("one who knows"). Tungusic is the language of the Tungusic peoples of Siberia and Northeast Asia, and Siberia is thought to be one of the primary originators of Shamanism.

Given the range of Shamanic practices worldwide, it is difficult to narrow down a clear definition of this religious practice. However, most scholars agree that Shamanism involves three major components:

- • Practitioners who alter the consciousness
- • A community that believes that altering one's consciousness is an important part of their religious rituals
- • Knowledge about the practice of altering one's consciousness for spiritual reasons is strictly controlled (especially by outsiders)

Most types of Shamanism can be divided into one of four categories:

1. Shamanism is a religious practice that involves anyone who contacts the spirit world while their state of consciousness is altered

2. Shamanism is a reference to the practice of contacting the spirit world. This is done while the Shaman is in a state of altered consciousness on behalf of someone else

3. Shamanism clearly means that Shamans are different from other people who can contact spirits, such as prophets, witch doctors, and mediums. What distinguishes Shamans is a question that has different answers in different cultures.

4. Shamanism strictly refers to the indigenous religions of Siberia and its neighboring regions in Asia. This category holds that, because Shamanism has its roots in Siberia, Siberian and Asian Shamanism is the only true version of this practice.

Shamanism usually focuses predominantly on Shamans, the main religious leaders of this practice. Shamans are people who have access to and who influence the spirit world. These people enter a state of altered consciousness during rituals, and this alteration in their consciousness helps them become successful as diviners and healers.

The Shaman is concerned with the health and well-being of the community at large. This doesn't just mean the people of their own community; it includes the entirety of the environment, including the plants and animals in and around the community.

As mentioned above, Shamans have access to the spirit world. They can visit this world by inducing an "ecstatic," altered state, leading to spiritual and physical transformations.

How a Shaman enters an ecstatic state depends on the traditions of the particular community being discussed. For example, South Americans and Siberian Shamans use hallucinogens (especially mushrooms, peyote, and alcohol) to enter this state. On the other hand, North American and Native American Shamans practice self-deprivation techniques, including isolation and fasting (among others).

## Types of Shamanism

As mentioned above, the oldest forms of Shamanism can be traced to Siberia. Siberian Shamanism involved the ingestion of the mushroom Amanita muscaria. Though this mushroom is poisonous, it is also extremely psychoactive, allowing consumers to enter an altered state of consciousness.

Following the classification of indigenous Siberian religious practices as *Shamanism*, it was quickly discovered that many other traditional practices fell under the broad umbrella of Shamanism as well. For this reason, Shamanism is often considered to be one of the oldest spiritual practices in the world.

### Siberian Shamanism

Siberian Shamanism involved consuming the fly agaric mushroom (Amanita muscaria) to reach the spirit world. The mushroom is poisonous in large quantities, and one of the distinguishing qualities of a skilled Shaman was the ability to identify the mushroom and consume the right amount of it *without overdosing.*

In Siberian Shamanism, the Shaman was one of the most revered members of a tribal group. Depending on the type of magic they specialized in, there were various Shamans. These included healers, black magic practitioners, spell workers, protectors (who would ward off evil spirits), and more.

The yurt - a portable round tend – played an important role in Siberian Shamanism (and Siberian beliefs in general) due to the nomadic nature of tribes in Siberia and Mongolia. It served as the connection between the physical plane and heavens and was designed to help Shamans travel the spirit and the cosmic worlds when they tried to contact the dead.

**South American Shamanism**

South American Shamanism primarily refers to the Shamanistic practices of Amazonian tribes. In these societies, the Shaman is often a chief-like figure closely associated with the jaguar. So close is this association that the word for "shaman" is similar or indistinguishable from the word for "jaguar" in many of these tribes.

This relationship is due to the fact that Shamans are believed to have the ability to transform into a jaguar when they want to. Jaguars, therefore, aren't considered to truly be animals. Rather, they are thought to either be a transformed Shaman or the soul of a dead Shaman visiting and traveling the physical realm.

To enter into an ecstatic state, South American Shamans drink tea made with a plant known as yagé (Banisteriopsis caapi). This plant contains a psychoactive compound (DMT). To give Shamans the ability to control the effect of the yagé, the tea usually includes another plant that contains a monoamine oxidase inhibitor. The plant that is chosen as this second ingredient often differs according to the tribe in question.

Aside from the yagé tea, South American Shamanism also emphasizes the ability of musical instruments (usually a drum or a rattle) to help Shamans enter an altered state. A rattle is the most common instrument that's used because it represents the awakened state that Shamans find themselves in when they travel to the spirit world. The gourd of the rattle is the universe, while the seeds inside are the souls of the ancestors. The handle represents the connection between the ancestors and the Shaman and is usually symbolic of the world tree that connects the cosmos.

## North American Shamanism

If popular North American literature were to be believed, every spiritual priest, healer, sorcerer, and ritual specialist would be a Shaman, or they would be practicing Shamanism. The term "Shamanism" is often used as a synonym for "primitive" religions, and a Shaman is, therefore, anyone who is considered a specialist in that religion.

However, in actual practice, North American Shamanism usually refers to a whole host of Native American religious practices rather than a single one. In North American Shamanism, Shamans typically come into their powers due to:

- Inheritance
- A personal quest (usually involving fasting or isolation)
- A spiritual gift
- Election by the tribe

However, no matter how they become Shamans, once they are given the title of "Shaman" and recognized as such, they are bestowed with enormous spiritual power.

Gaining Shamanic power is usually followed by a quest for a spirit guide. This spirit guide can take many forms, including:

- Mythological figures
- Deities
- A ghost of an ancestor
- A soul of a living thing
- Animals

Animal Spirit Guides are perhaps the most common and most well-known of these.

The form a spirit guide takes is significant, as each form has its unique symbolism. Among the most revered forms is that of the eagle.

Most Native American tribes hold a special reverence for eagles, and they are considered sacred in Native American tradition and religion. They are representative of courage and strength, truth and honesty, wisdom, power, and freedom.

They are thought to have a special connection with the Creator. The Creator is believed to have chosen the eagle as the leader of all birds as it flies higher and sees better than other birds. This gives eagles a unique perspective of things. It spends more time in the Sky than other birds, and the Sky is thought to be an element of the Spirit.

The eagle is thought to carry messages to the Creator by taking them from this world to the spirit world, where the Creator lives. All of these factors also mean that Native American tribes place a special significance on eagle feathers.

Being given an eagle feather is considered the highest honor in many tribes, with the feather of the golden eagle being the most significant. Eagle feathers can be given for various reasons, and they were traditionally presented to braves, chiefs, and warriors following extreme acts of bravery.

Additionally, many traditional dancers use eagle feathers in their dance regalia. This is especially common in Creek and Cherokee tribes, as both cultures have Eagle Dances that represent strength and power.

Eagle feathers are also seen in Native American headdresses. Each feather represents a different act of bravery, and the more eagle feathers in a given headdress, the more honored the person wearing it is. Eagle feathers are earned one at a time, which helps explain the importance of the number of feathers a person may possess.

The importance of the eagle in Native American culture helps explain why an eagle spirit guide was often regarded as important. Eagles are not the only guide that has an inherent meaning - Native American Shamanism believed that each different guide had its own symbolism.

Additionally, North American Shamans also make use of "power objects," which display their spiritual power and help them make contact with the spirit world. In some cases, power objects may also refer to specific charms, formulas, and songs used by a Shaman.

The primary duty and function of a Native American Shaman are healing. Native American belief states that there are usually two major causes of disease:

- **Object Intrusion** is when an object that can affect your health enters your body. This is often a result of sorcery and witchcraft, though this is not always the case.
- **Soul Loss** – the exact theories differ based on the tribe, but this condition usually involves the soul (or life force) of a person leaving their body for various reasons (including theft by a malevolent being).

Each of these conditions can be treated using the powers of a Shaman. Object intrusion is treated by sucking out the offending object utilizing an instrument such as a tube or horn. Soul loss can be combated using magical flights, spirit journeys, and chanting.

Other duties that Shamans can handle include:

- Weather control
- Functions related to hunting, including game divination and charming
- General divination practices, including foretelling the future and finding lost objects
- War-related functions

While Native American Shamans are usually benevolent, this isn't always true. Shamans are often considered "potentially malevolent" and can use their abilities for sorcery, revenge, or witchcraft (for themselves or others), depending on their personal belief system.

In general, most Native American Shamans are men. However, some tribes in Northern California do have a tradition of female Shamans.

## Shamanic Beliefs

While each indigenous tribe and group has its own Shamanic beliefs, some common themes can be seen across cultures. These include:

- **A belief that everything is interrelated and interconnected**. If one person or species suffers, so does everyone (and everything) else. Thus, the health of humanity is connected to the health of the rest of the web of life. Furthermore, the Shaman must serve as a bridge between these two (human and nature).

- **There are two aspects to the natural world** – ordinary, everyday awareness, which consists of things we see and believe, and non-ordinary awareness, which can only be accessed through an altered state. The universe can seem non-linear and fluid in this second state of consciousness. This state is spirit-oriented, while the ordinary reality is matter-oriented.

- **Everything is alive and possesses a spirit**. This belief is known as animism and includes both humans and animals and non-living things such as streams, mountains, and other natural phenomena. Shamanism allows Shamans to see these spirits, which usually reside in the invisible, spirit world.

- **Shamans can access other realms by altering their consciousness**, and this altered state allows Shamans to transport their souls to the non-ordinary, invisible world.

9

This is known as a *Shamanic journey*, which we'll explore in detail below.

- **The non-ordinary reality accessible to Shamans is "more real" than the ordinary reality everyone can experience**. In the non-ordinary reality, Shamans can obtain clarity about events in the ordinary reality. Because understanding can be obtained in this invisible reality, journeying there is also referred to as "going to the source." This, in turn, makes it "more real" than the ordinary reality, which is an offshoot of the "source," or the spirit world.

- **There are three planes (or realms) of consciousness,** linked by a vertical axis known as the Axis Mundi, the World Tree, or the Tree of Life. Shamans use this axis to travel across realms.

- **Shamanic ritual is meant to use the spirit world to bring about change** in the physical world. The spirit world (non-ordinary reality) and the physical world (ordinary reality) interact continuously, and Shamans can learn how to change the physical world by taking action in the spirit world.

- **Shamanism is based on the idea that Shamans can access inner wisdom** and guidance through the experience of ecstatic trances. Shamanism allows practitioners to experience revelations that come from within themselves. It involves developing your true self and places emphasis on the uniqueness of the individual.

## Tree of Life

As mentioned above, the Tree of Life is the axis that connects the Three Shamanic Worlds, and it is what Shamans use to travel between the worlds. It's essential for Shamans to keep in mind that this axis can take many forms, depending on the tradition of

Shamanism they are practicing – the Tree of Life is simply the most common form.

Shamans will first gather strength while they wait at the foot of the Tree of Life. Through practice, they can develop a constantly growing power source here, which they can access during their journeys. Once a Shaman has gathered enough power, they can begin their journey through the Three Worlds.

## Three Shamanic Worlds

There are Three Shamanic Worlds or three spirit worlds that Shamans can travel to the Underworld, the Middle World, and the Upper World. Some traditions may divide these worlds further into subcategories, but these three worlds are common across most – if not all – Shamanic beliefs.

Each world has its own atmosphere and vibration, and travel to these worlds is usually done with a power animal or a spirit helper. A rattle or a trance rhythm usually accompanies it, and Shamans will usually use the Axis Mundi/Tree of Life as a "road" to guide them through the worlds.

**1. Underworld**: In Shamanism, the underworld is located underground. It exists at the roots of the Axis Mundi, and Shamans must descend deep under the earth to get there. They usually travel to the underground via a tunnel or corridor that can be entered once they reach the base of the tree, but it can also take the form of:

- A narrow slit
- An animal hole
- A staircase
- An opening at the mouth of a waterfall
- An opening in the earth

The underworld has a connection to power and transformation, and the spirit helpers that Shamans encounter in the underworld will usually take the form of animals. The underworld is usually where the Shamans go when they want to perform healing and transformation rituals and personal work and resources.

**2. Middle World**: The middle world looks similar to the earthly, ordinary reality that everyone can see. However, it includes more than just the physical reality – it also includes the spiritual reality of the earthly dimension. It includes everything beyond the veils of ordinary perception, such as the souls of nature and the past and future of everything on Earth. Shamans travel to the middle world to gather specific information that they need, usually pertaining to a place or event on earth. They will also travel to the middle world if they want to work in a certain space and need to contact the soul of that place. The middle world usually forms the trunk of the Tree of Life.

**3. Upper World:** Located high above the earthly/middle world, the upper world can be reached by traveling higher, usually accompanied by a powerful animal or spirit helper. The Shaman takes a "flight of the spirit" to reach this realm. The spirit helpers of the upper world are often different from those of the underworld and help provide the Shaman with a different perspective and distance from difficult situations.

## Journeying

As mentioned above, journeying involves a Shaman traveling from the physical realm and ordinary reality to non-ordinary reality (the spirit realm).

This ritual is always performed in the context of a sacred ceremony and should not be taken lightly. By entering an altered state of consciousness, Shamans on these journeys can communicate with helpful spirits and retrieve important information, usually for healing purposes.

Shamans can embark on a journey through a trance induced with the help of rhythmic percussion (via a drum or rattle) or Shaman songs. They may also ingest plant medicine or psychoactive to help them on this journey. The plants they ingest are often considered to be spiritual entities in themselves, and common options include:

- Ayahuasca
- Iboga
- San Pedro cactus
- Any of a range of psychedelic mushrooms
- Salvia
- Peyote

During a journey, the Shaman is often accompanied by helpful spirits. These spirits can take a variety of forms and are often either spirit guides or power animals.

- Spirit guides tend to take a human or humanoid form and help guide Shamans through unfamiliar realms. They are teachers, protectors, and companions all-in-one. Some Shamans may enter into a spiritual marriage with their spirit guide, and they are often also considered to be gods and ancestors of the community they want to help.
- According to Shamanism, every person – whether Shaman or not – is born with the spirit of one or more animals. These animals serve as guides. One of these often serves as a power animal, which helps protect and guide Shamans on their journey and lends them wisdom and attributes. For example, a jaguar power animal will teach the Shaman to walk fearlessly in the dark.

The Shamanic journey is a key part of Shamanism, and the Shaman's ability to undertake these journeys is part of why they are so highly revered.

In the next chapter, we'll look at the power animals and Animal Spirit Guides that accompany Shamans on their journey in more detail and examine the role that totem animals play in Shamanism.

# Chapter 2: Animal Spirit Guides vs. Power Animals vs. Totems

Growing up, we've all heard the term "spirit animal" on multiple occasions. We've seen it on TV shows, in movies, and in stories. You've probably even taken a quiz in one of those teen magazines or on an online platform to find out what your spirit animal is. But what exactly is a spirit animal? Is it the same as an Animal Spirit Guide? Is it the animal that represents your mind and soul the most? Were you that animal in your past life? Will you be reincarnated as one after you die?

There are many misconceptions when it comes to the world of animism. While it sounds reasonable to say that one's spirit animal is simply the animal they are inside or even the animal they'd be if they weren't human, this explanation is not nearly accurate. In fact, while it's still not entirely accurate, this serves as a slightly better definition for the term "power animal."

If you're new to Shamanism and spirituality, the chances are that you're feeling confused. The terms "Animal Spirit Guides, "power animals," and "animal totem" are often used interchangeably, even though they are all different things. This often results in a lot of confusion, inaccuracy, and misguidance. These symbols or energies have something different and significant to teach us. Each of them plays a distinct role and shows up in various forms and situations, and they show up for certain purposes with specific messages or lessons to teach. Getting to know what each term stands for and what you need each spiritual being for can make it much easier to work with the medicines and energies of each.

In this chapter, we will help you understand the role of animals in our lives. By understanding the difference between Animal Spirit Guides, power animals, and animal totems, you'll know how to use their energies for self-growth, development, and healing. After reading this chapter, you'll have a better sense of why and when you can turn to each animal to help you in your life.

## Animal Spirit Guide

An Animal Spirit Guide, as you may have guessed, is there to guide you. These guides step forward in difficult situations and challenging periods of our lives to help us identify the lessons we need to learn. Animal Spirit Guides allow us to make sense of our experiences.

These guides teach us to stay grounded and attain a sense of stability and peacefulness, both spiritually and in the physical world. Each animal has a different power and skill set, which is why we can all have more than one Animal Spirit Guide in our lifetimes. The animal that chooses us shares its knowledge with us so we can effectively deal with the challenges of life and the manifestations we encounter on our spiritual journeys.

Your Animal Spirit Guide will reveal itself in the most natural and humble way possible. Whether you consciously and specifically call on it for guidance or you are in dire need of help and support, your spirit animal will appear to you in moments of unconsciousness or where you least expect them. Once they do, you need to work incessantly to find out what message they're trying to deliver.

The number of Animal Spirit Guides you have in your life depends on the number of lessons you need to learn and the obstacles you must endure in a lifetime. If you tend to fall into the same traps repeatedly, you may have one Animal Spirit Guide accompany you throughout your entire life. Otherwise, they may make an appearance just to guide you through one specific challenge.

Several types of Animal Spirit Guides may show up at different times during your life.

## The Crossroads

The Crossroads Animal Spirit Guide is also known as Journey Animal Spirit. This animal spirit comes into your life when you are at a "crossroads" or have a major life decision to make. These guides typically appear when you're taking a new path in life. Their mission is to ensure that you walk down the right life path and make the best out of your journey. These guides stick by their chosen human until they've successfully made it through the current challenge and walked confidently down the new life path.

## The Medicine Animal Spirit

In Shamanism, the word "Medicine" refers to the healing energies that animal spirits carry. In the end, Animal Spirit Guides come into our lives in times of great need. They offer reassurance, comfort, guidance, support, and most importantly, they help us learn and heal from past traumas and ongoing challenges. Animal Spirit Guides help us become the best versions of ourselves and unlock our full potential. However, what's so special about the Medicine Animal Spirit is that its healing abilities can extend to comfort and cure us when we're suffering from severe injuries and illnesses. However, they only respond to the call of professional or experienced healers and Shamans. The Medicine Animal Spirit Guide will stick by your side until you are recovered and feel ready to take on the rest of your journey on your own. Besides their incredible healing abilities, these guides are brimming with great wisdom. They will offer you all the guidance you need to emerge stronger from your healing journey.

**The Shadow Animal**

The Shadow Animal, another type of Animal Spirit Guide, comes into your life before you have learned the lessons you are destined to learn. The Shadow Animal appears when you insistently ignore all opportunities that life throws at you. They also come into your life whenever you seem stuck in a certain behavioral pattern that doesn't serve you, or they show up before a life lesson. This behavior may cause your life lessons to manifest over and over again, preventing you from moving forward with your life. You can expect the Shadow Animal to appear multiple times until a change is made. These guides usually manifest in times of great perplexity and adversity. The confusion comes from the fact that it makes its presence known in unique ways, unlike the rest of the guides. They are called "Shadow" Animals for a reason, after all. Shadow Animals can guide you back to the light after you've lost your way in the darkness. They only appear when you hit rock bottom.

Animal Spirit Guides may appear in your life to improve your affinity and bond over multiple occasions. If you notice their disappearance before everything falls into place, you need to rethink your behavior. They may leave if they sense a lack of appreciation or disrespect. There are ways you can remedy the situation. However, realizing what *exactly went wrong* is a must.

Animal Spirit Guides can also leave one's life if they believe that another guide can offer better guidance in a specific area or situation. They may also leave because they have already taught you everything there is to teach and offered all their skills, making it time to learn from another guide. Some Animal Spirit Guides are seasonal, meaning that they are there to guide you through cyclical energies. In that case, the Animal Spirit Guide will differ from season to season.

Animal Spirit Guides don't always show up in times of need, and they can simply make an appearance during special occasions or happy events, bringing more positivity with them.

Messages that Animal Spirit Guides deliver to us are extremely personal. The best way to deduce the message is by paying attention to your thoughts when the animal comes to mind. Let's say your Animal Spirit Guide is a lion and that you immediately think of the lion's roar when you conjure a mental image of it. In this case, the message may have to do with using your voice, expressing yourself, and communicating with others. If you associate the animal with negative things, you can think of the risky aspects of your life. Do you have any habits, partake in any activities, or are taking on any ventures that may need you to have increased protection and awareness? If you don't have any opinions or knowledge about the creature, you can look into its symbolic meaning, religious connotations, or associated folklore.

Every animal has a certain theme or underlying energy. Horses, for instance, are generally associated with freedom, endurance, determination, and spirit. Do these elements revolve around a specific circumstance or situation in your life? Perhaps you've always wanted to relocate or start over elsewhere, but you doubt your decision. This could be your sign to move forward with your plan. If you're still unsure what the message may be, try understanding the animal's nature and practicing activities that mimic its behavior. This can help strengthen your connection to the creature and, therefore, speak in a somewhat similar language to it.

**Power Animals**

Power animals can seem a lot like Animal Spirit Guides at first. We call upon our power animals in times of extreme need, powerlessness, and fear. You can think of them as guardians, supporters, or protectors when facing obstacles or challenges in life.

They have a plethora of skills and unique powers that can help you acquire the strength and courage you need to make it through tough times.

They serve as guides and protectors, which explains why one might confuse them for Animal Spirit Guides. However, what's different about power animals is that they represent each of our traits, soul, characteristics, and personality. Unlike spirit animals, one's power animal accompanies them from birth. While Animal Spirit Guides show up in our lives at certain moments for specific reasons, power animals are always there to guide us, protect us, and empower us throughout our entire lives. Our power animals are the ones that choose us, as well.

Their meaning, innate symbolism, and traits determine how the power animals will use their gifts to guide us. After connecting with your power animal, you can tap into its instincts and characteristics and channel them into your daily duties and interactions. We can derive a great deal of strength and courage from our power animals to withstand the challenging transitions in life. We can manifest the powers of our power animals and allow them to inspire us to move on from the bad experiences and take on new and better ones.

## Animal Spirit Guides vs. Power Animals

In a much simpler sense, modern Western Shamanic beliefs explain that Animal Spirit Guides resemble personal protectors and can provide individual guidance. They come in at several points to help us make it through different trials.

Meanwhile, power animals are animal spirits that choose to connect with a specific person and unite with their spirit. This is why there are plenty of common characteristics and personality traits between an individual and their power animal. This resemblance makes it easier for a person to draw on their power animal's strength and manifest it in their daily life. If there weren't some sort of common ground, it would be extremely hard for us to learn, benefit from, and relate to our power animals.

Our power animals are our source of strength and support, and we turn to them when obstacles arise or whenever we need the courage to face challenges head-on. The animal's power, energy, skills, and survival instincts inspire us to push forward and find our inner strength.

## Totem Animals

In most cases, a "totem animal" is just another name given to the "power animal." You'll even find many sources referring to power and totem animals as one. However, you should know that totemism is very eminent in different parts of the world.

So, what are totems? Totems are sacred symbols, objects, or spiritual beings that serve as tokens for groups of people. These groups can be clans, families, tribes, or lineages. While some elements of religion, such as rituals, are apparent in totemism, it is not essentially a religion, and neither is it Ancestor Worship.

There are two types of Totemism.

## Group Totemism

There are several characteristics of Group Totemism. For one, it wholly recognizes an animal, phenomena, or plant as significant to a lineage, tribe, family, or clan. The connection between a group and their Totem may go as deep as them believing that the totem is their ancestor, and wondrous myths may form due to this belief.

Groups may describe their Totem as possessing magical powers and shapeshifting abilities. Besides their protection, healing, and guiding energies, groups may believe that their Totem can take on a human visage, which typically earns a Totem great respect. Since some taboos or concepts are tied to Totemism, different groups tend to have shared activities, beliefs, and behaviors.

## Individual Totemism

Individual Totemism reflects the Individual deep connections with animal spirits and energies, and it is a clear expression of this bond. Humans who partake in Individual Totemism believe that the Totem gives them power, which is very similar to the definition or purpose of power animals. The person's relationship with their Totem Animals is similar to a soul contract; it is decided *long before the individual's birth*, and both souls work together in harmony.

As you know, no one chooses their Totem Animal. The animal chooses its human and makes its presence known at the right moment. When the person becomes aware of their Totem Animal and the nature of their relationship, and the characteristics and traits of their Totem, they are presented with more opportunities for growth and development. There is nothing like the connection between a human and their Totem Animal. It is quite sacred.

Our connection with animals is one thing that most people have started paying less attention to over time. Unfortunately, we've grown more and more disconnected from nature with all the technological advances and the fast-paced nature of life. At times, we even take nature and the relationship we can form with it for granted.

We need to learn from our ancestors the importance of staying grounded and blending in with our surroundings. Many ancient civilizations, especially ones that tried to make sense of the world through nature and spirituality, believed that we need to seek guidance and aid from animals during our lifetimes.

# PART TWO: Shamanic Animal Work

# Chapter 3: Discovering Your Animal Spirit Guides

Numerous ancient societies and tribes were highly aware of Animal Spirit Guides' power. They acknowledged the importance of creating harmonious relationships and connections with these Guides. As you're probably aware by now, Shamanic traditions in different world areas showed that each animal has its own distinctive spirit and energy. They trusted that we could call for the Animal Spirits to Guide us through our life's journey. Their power can protect, help, and heal us throughout our lives. Shamans believe that these Guides are not just a source of power, but they are also teachers and allies who can offer significant aid and insight into one's life.

Chief Dan George of Tsleil-Waututh, who was also an actor, poet, musician, and author, once said that you should always remember to talk to animals because if you do, they'll answer you. If you don't speak to them, they will not reply, and you will not have their insight. When you lack insight and understanding, you will feel fearful, and perhaps, destroy the animals. Ultimately, when you destroy the animals, you destroy yourself in the process.

Shamans usually find themselves in trances where they can meet their guides, and some practices require Shamans to find their specific Animal Spirit Guide. Your specific Animal Spirit Guide could either be your best fit or one that has been previously separated from you. *You should know that you don't get to choose your Animal Spirit Guide;* instead, they get to choose you. However, as we explained throughout the previous chapters, you can have more than one Animal Spirit Guide during your lifetime.

Finding your spirit animal can transform your life in ways you can't imagine. These positive changes can impact your spiritual, mental, emotional, and physical health. You can think of this communication as a medicinal or energy guide. There's a choice that every individual must make if they're lucky enough to discover their Animal Spirit Guide. They can decide to accept and welcome their messages or completely ignore them.

Accepting and acting on your Animal Spirit Guide's messages can be quite rewarding. The lessons and guidance that they'll pour into your life can be similar to a spiritual awakening. You'll find that everything, including friendships, romantic partners, professional relationships, thought and behavioral patterns, culinary, fashion, artistic, and musical tastes, and careers that don't serve you will disappear from your life. You'll only be surrounded by things and people that serve your best interests.

Finding your Animal Spirit Guide can help you realize and connect with the non-material aspects of life. It can be your opportunity to sharpen all your 6 senses and hone your natural thinking abilities and instincts. When finding your Animal Spirit Guides, the most important thing is readiness. You have to want to transform your life for the better. You need to be ready to let go of everything that doesn't serve you and embrace the positive changes. You shouldn't overthink this, though, because if you're reading this book, then the chances are that you're ready to embark on this journey.

This chapter will discuss the importance of discovering your Animal Spirit Guide. We'll help you find out what it is and how to call upon it. You'll learn the best time to do so, as well as potential signs that they may be present.

## Why You Should Discover Your Animal Spirit Guide

As we explained above, finding your Animal Spirit Guide can bless your life with many rewarding changes. Your guide can help you navigate rapid waters and rough patches. It can also help rid you of everything that no longer serves you and guide you toward more beneficial opportunities. Essentially, your Spirit Guide can give you the courage you need to leave toxic relationships or environments. It will also give you the confidence you need to stand up for yourself and ask for things you believe you deserve, such as raises or promotions. You will not be afraid to go to new places or start new chapters if it serves your greater good, such as leaving your hometown for college or a job opportunity.

Communicating with your Spirit Guides can teach you how to properly express yourself and speak up about the things that truly matter to you. It will also pave the way toward aligning with your intuitive and psychic self. Your Animal Spirit Guides can give you the strength to make it through the hardest moments in life –struggling with addiction, depression, and other mental illnesses or simply having a hard time finding your passions and happiness in life. Most importantly, your Animal Spirit Guide will give you the wisdom you need to make life-changing decisions. We need our spirit animal guides the most whenever we feel sad, fearful, or angry.

## Discovering Your Animal Spirit Guides

According to several ancient beliefs, each person's character has nine significant positions filled by Animal Spirit Guides. The first four

Animal Spirit Guides take up the four directions: North, South, East, and West. Every direction they occupy can be considered a window to your personal development and growth. It is also a bridge to grasping a deeper understanding of yourself, essence, and everything around you.

## North

The Spirit Guide that occupies the Northern direction typically teaches you when to listen and when to speak up. It is there to provide you with wisdom and encourage you to express yourself. You may be surprised to learn that this guide can often block your efforts, forcing you to take a moment to listen to others. These guides teach us how to be thankful.

## South

These guides are responsible for helping you find emotional intelligence and wisdom. They essentially help us reconnect with our inner child and reclaim our authentic selves, even after having experienced the ever-changing dynamics of life. These guides can help us determine which people to trust, when to trust them, and under which circumstances. They can also help us learn the nature of humility.

## East

These guides brighten up our personal paths. They travel with us on all our journeys to help clarify certain situations and tackle spiritual challenges. They are responsible for our spiritual awakening.

## West

They can help us search deep within ourselves to find our fundamental truths. They can lead us to internal answers and enable us to recognize our intuitions and goals. These are generally the guides that someone needs to seek while experiencing a midlife crisis.

## Above

The Animal Spirit Guide that occupies the above position can help you have faith in the Great Universal Spirit. It will help you pick up on the messages that you get on your journey and are intended to help you or aid others. This is the Spirit Guide that teaches you to honor your higher power and safeguards your subconscious mind.

**Below**

This Animal Spirit Guide can help you find your way to Mother Earth. Through this guide, you will learn how to stay grounded and understand why you need to do it as you experience life. You will find it hard to follow your designated path if you're not grounded. This guide can save you from losing your way and help you to avoid any confusion and lack of focus. This Animal Guide's task is not easy.

**Inside**

This Animal Spirit Guide, as you may have guessed, is supposed to protect your inner being. They are there to protect your true self. They are there to remind you that you're the only person who knows your real self. They are also responsible for helping you realize the work you need to do to develop. They'll help you find joy even when the weight of the world is on your shoulders.

**Right Side**

This is often identified as the male side and will likely appear at your door first. They're recognized as courageous, protective spirits. The Right Side Guide will teach you how to find and muster the courage to face your fears and challenges that the outside world may throw at you.

**Left Side**

The Left Side Guides usually show up after the Right Side ones and are identified as the female side. They are associated with nurturing us and teaching us about all the related aspects of life. These guides hold a mother's unconditional love and can help teach us how to adapt to different life situations and deal with relationships.

## Finding Your Animal Spirit Guide

We've already established that you don't choose your Animal Spirit Guide but that it chooses you. Spirit Guides can show up in your life unexpectedly. However, if you can't see the signs, you need to ask it to reveal itself to you. You need to keep in mind that this practice is sacred and that it can take you a while to find your guide. You need to stay focused and determined. Try not to lose hope because, like anything else, finding your Animal Spirit Guide won't happen overnight.

Before you start seeking your guide, try paying attention to the signs. Is there a certain animal that you've been running into repeatedly? Think about physical encounters, symbolic forms, pictures, or stories. Animal Spirit Guides tend to show up insistently on several occasions. While you may not pay much attention to these encounters at first, the answer becomes obvious once you think about it. Let's say your Animal Spirit Guide is a horse. At the beginning of the week, your child brings home a "fun fact book" about horses from school. Then, you open the TV to find National Geographic streaming a documentary on wild horses. A few days later, you come across a sign for nearby horse-riding lessons, and suddenly, "Spirit: Stallion of the Cimarron" is recommended on all your streaming services. The horse's medicine and spirit are trying to communicate with you.

You can also think back to your childhood as the Right and Left Side Animal Spirit Guides tend to show up during the earlier stages of our lives. Did you have frequent dreams – or even nightmares – about an animal as you were growing up? Perhaps you were inexplicably attached to a certain animal during your childhood. Think back to the times you spent at zoos or animal sanctuaries. Was there a specific animal that you spent most of your visits watching? Did you own several books or watch a lot of movies about it? Maybe you've always held a deep liking to a certain animal or encountered it recurrently during your early life. The first animal that showed up in this pattern is your Right Side Guide, and the second animal is your Left Side Guide.

When we grow older, the Animal Spirit can show up when we need guidance in one of the other seven areas that we discussed above. For instance, during periods when we struggle with the direction of faith, the Above Animal Spirit Guide may show up. They can appear when you ask for help or meditate or dream, and they can also show up on multiple occasions in your life.

If you want to find your Animal Spirit Guide, let it come to you while meditating, dreaming, or in other states of consciousness. Make sure you ask the animal to appear to you or at least set the intention before you go to sleep or start meditating. If you're into other spiritual activities, you can try to find your Animal Spirit Guide through tarot cards, decks, or books. You can seek help from professional energy healers or Shamans if you want.

The best you can do is start slowly if you want to do this independently. Before you jump right into visualization meditation, you can try to improve your focus during the day. Try setting your intention by repeating phrases that signify your readiness to find your Animal Spirit Guide and your openness to receiving everything it has to share with you. Then, pay attention to every encounter that you have with animals. Though, you shouldn't be quick to attempt interaction with it. The best you can do is allow it to appear to you in its purest spiritual form. If it's your guide, it will come to you. This process has to be executed with pure intuitiveness and modesty.

## Visualization Meditation

Once you're ready, you can try a visualization meditation to find your Animal Spirit Guide. To do so, you must steer clear of any distractions and technology. Try to surround yourself with nature. You can either lie down or sit on the bare ground with your eyes closed. Try to pay your undivided attention to the direction in which the wind blows and the sounds of nature, whether they're birds, leaves, raindrops, or other animals, around you. Don't resist your thoughts and simply allow them to slide through your mind. Don't try to connect or hold onto any thought, either. Just watch them flip through your brain.

Focus on your breath, and don't try to control it. Don't slow it down or speed it up and just allow it to flow in and out naturally. Feel your body as it sinks deeper into the ground underneath you. Then, begin to visualize a doorway in a forest right in front of you. Picture yourself taking one step closer toward the door with each breath you take. When you are ready, pull the door wide open and embrace the auditory and emotional changes. You should be in the utter void. You may feel scared and lost; however, just then, you will feel an accompanying presence.

This presence will not scare you because it will feel quite familiar, and you will feel safe and protected. This guiding energy has come to introduce yourself to you, and it is here to reassure you that you're not lost. When it offers you its protection, you will come to understand that it's your spiritual guide.

You may be wondering if it's a young and small spirit or a large and old one. This is when you need to reach deep into your pockets to fetch a flashlight. Inhale deeply, turn it on, and be ready to see your Animal Spirit Guide. You can reach your fingertips out to touch it. Take as much time as you need to connect to it and bond with it. Feel it illuminate your essence. Don't open your eyes until you're ready to do so.

## Communicating with Your Animal Spirit Guide

When communicating with your Animal Spirit Guide, try to forget that you're human. Take the time to learn about its characteristics and traits. Make sure to learn about the animal, its behaviors, tendencies, communication style, and environment. When you become familiar with its habitat, its senses, the sounds it makes, and the skills it can use, you'll find it easier to think like it. Ponder what this animal has to teach and what it is protective over. This is all needed so you can become receptive and responsive to the messages it's trying to send you. Remember to use your intuition and unlock all your spiritual gifts in the process. You need to be serious about your desire to make changes and find the path to personal growth. Your growing desire and determination will improve communication, and it can bring back more helpful and clearer messages from your guide.

Keep in mind that it can take you days, weeks, or even months to understand what your Animal Spirit Guide is trying to tell you. It might take you even longer to resolve the issue. To get by, think of your Animal Spirit Guide as a companion. Think of this as an experience rather than a task.

**Signs It Is Present**
- Seeing white feathers
- Coming across pennies and dimes
- Flowery or nostalgic scents
- Dreams and orbs
- Song lyrics that answer your questions
- Light touches and gentle chills

Animal Spirit Guides enter and exit our lives as we seek guidance. They teach us valuable lessons about ourselves and aid us in achieving and maintaining balance. The Animal Spirit Guide that makes its way into our journey is determined by the timing of events, the direction we're headed, the tasks we need to complete, events that come our way, and the different phases of our lives. These Spirit Guides don't communicate their message in a specific way or form. They can show up in our dreams, cross paths with us, appear in our meditation, or we can even have them as pets.

# Chapter 4: Meeting Your Power Animal

Many Power Animals can offer their gifts to you, but there is only one you can forge a lifelong spiritual connection with. Finding the animal that helps you discover yourself, heals you, and supports you on your life's journey is imperative for a successful Shamanic journey. This chapter will shed light on the different ways you can discover your Power Animal. The knowledge you gain will be particularly empowering if you struggle to find your Power Animal or have suffered Soul Loss. However, it's important to note that you should only use your Power Animal as a means to connect to the spiritual world and not for Soul Retrieval. The latter is considered an advanced Shamanic ritual that can only be practiced safely after gathering the highest level of wisdom and power.

## Understanding the Nature of Power Animals

Understanding how a Power Animal can enrich your Shamanic practice is the first step toward finding the right animal. This is a being that you will be building a lifelong connection with - and to be able to rely on their gifts, you will need to know what they can bring to your life. As a newcomer to the world of Shamanic practice, you may find Power Animal Retrieval quite challenging. People usually notice the physical strength of animals, whereas Shamans and Shamanic practitioners can look beyond the physical manifestation of power to uncover spiritual qualities as well. You may even feel drawn to an animal's spirit, and you aren't even aware of it. To be able to retrieve their power, you must fully commit to understanding the nature of your Power Animal.

## How to Meet Your Power Animal

It isn't just people who are drawn to their spiritual guides. Power Animals feel the same pull towards their human counterparts. So, without a doubt, yours will want to meet you just as much as you want to retrieve them. Your Power Animal will signal their readiness to accompany you on your Shamanic journey, and they may do this in several ways. Your Power Animal will choose to appear - you will just have to be vigilant about your surroundings to notice them when they do. You can also perform a Power Animal Retrieval through Shamanic journeys if you need immediate assistance. This is a more productive approach for meeting the animal that can guide you through the Spirit World. Whichever way you try to meet them, you must remember that this is a sacred journey that you need to take without any prejudice or expectation.

## A Shamanic Lower World Journey

A Shamanic Lower World journey is usually recommended as the second journey in Shamanic practices. It's also one of the most efficient ways to meet and connect with your Power Animal. To begin this journey, you must relax and state your intention of finding your Power Animal. You can do this by focusing your mind on your mission and communicating your desire to the world by saying it out loud. Envision a place in nature where you usually feel the most comfortable and use this as your anchor spot. When you have conjured up this spot, you can start looking for the way to get down into the Lower World. This could be any place in nature, so pay attention to your surroundings in the vision. Once you have located the natural feature you are looking for, prepare to move into the nature-based Lower World. Keep in mind that while the entrance may seem impossible to use, you are entering into a spiritual world. This means that you are receiving spiritual gifts that will allow you to enter the Lower World. By making the path harder, the spirits are testing if you are ready to join them, and the only way to prove your readiness is by using the provided entrance, no matter how uncomfortable it is.

Once you arrive, you may be surprised at the appearance of the Lower World. Even if you have heard about other people's experiences before, it's a journey that leads every Shamanic practitioner to a different path. While it may be tempting to look around, staying close to the entrance and waiting for your Power Animal to come to you is recommended. If more than one animal approaches you, reach out to them through your spirit and try to feel which one is yours. Usually, once the right animal gets close enough, both of you will feel a pull towards each other's spirit.

Some Shamans suggest waiting until you see four of the same animals roaming around the entrance to ensure it's your Power Animal. Others say you must ask the animal you feel drawn to if it's your Power Animal. It will communicate its answer verbally, telepathically, or by acting it out. If the answer is no, wait until the next animal comes along and repeat the process. You may get several negative answers in a row, but it's all part of the journey. Don't be discouraged even if you can't retrieve your Power Animal during your first journey either; this just means that you weren't ready to meet it yet, or you didn't need its guidance at the time.

It's also a good idea to keep an open mind about which animal may be your spiritual guide. People often feel drawn to more than one animal at a time because they have not committed to one yet. Furthermore, you may think you need more guidance, so you set your mind on the strongest Power Animal. However, each animal has their unique quality, and you will be partnered with the one whose gift you need the most. When you arrive in the Lower World, you must be ready to meet any animal that presents itself as your Power Animal. Preparing yourself will ensure that you aren't missing out on the guidance you require. Remember, the spirits know what you need, and they will send you the animal that will provide you with it.

Once your Power Animal has chosen to accompany you, you may begin to explore the Lower World with its guidance. As it's unfamiliar territory with many confusing paths, it's a good idea to stay close to your Power Animal. This way, when you hear the callback, the animal will show you the way to the entrance, even if you fail to remember it.

## Alternative Ways to Meet Your Power Animal

Besides a journey to the Lower World, Shamanic practitioners can also choose other ways to do a Power Animal Retrieval. Here are some alternative ways to meet your Animal Spirit Guide.

### Comparing Traits

If you feel drawn to more than one Power Animal, it's because they have all presented themselves to you, but you weren't able to commit to any of them. The culprit for this is usually your inability to find the proper spiritual connection with your Power Animal. As mentioned before, when looking for an animal, you must look beyond their physical abilities and seek out the spiritual gift they are offering. Power Animals are the personification of your own spirit, and you will only be able to connect to the one whose spirit resembles your inner self the most. The identity of your Power Animal is based on your emotional needs and the personality traits you need to improve. By enlightening you with a specific lesson, your animal is making you stronger emotionally and physically - but the change always comes from within. By comparing your personality traits to animal characteristics, you can discover the animal you can rely on for lifelong spiritual guidance. Knowing you inside out, they can act better as a guide, a teacher, a protector, an ally, or a messenger in the Spiritual World.

## Meditation

Like a Shamanic journey to the nature-based Lower World, meditation is another great way to free your mind and let your Power Animal come to you. Mediation focuses on regulating your breathing which allows you to relax, effectively clearing any internal interferences from your spiritual journey. In this relaxed state, it will be much easier to sense your Power Animal and connect to them spiritually. When you feel that your mind is free of prejudice, think of an animal you feel drawn to. Often, the first answer that comes to mind is your Power Animal. If you don't have much experience with mediation, you may ask an experienced guide to lead you on this path. You can try a similar exercise through channeled writing as well. After relaxing your mind, write down any signs or animals you have noticed around you. When you have finished, read your notes, and you will see the signs of Your Power Animal appearing in them quite frequently.

## Paying Attention to Signs

Beyond showing themselves in their physical form, each Power Animal communicates their intentions through various other means. It will send you signs and symbols you may receive via any of your senses - whether you are awake or dreaming. This will most likely happen under unique circumstances where the messages will be hard to miss. You have a close kinship with your Power Animal, so it will appear to help you out when you need its guidance. You may not see the animal walking around, but you will hear its message in the song's lyrics or dream about it frequently. The Power Animal may appear as a vision whenever you seek support or confirmation of your ideas. The more you begin to pay attention to the subtle hints it sends you, the easier it will be to accept its help. Just remember that you must look for natural signs and not artificial ones.

## Asking for Signs

If you require guidance in a pressing matter, you can ask your Power Animal to show itself to you physically as a direct answer to your question. Doing it multiple times will signal to the animal that you really need its help, and it will come to your aid. Seeing an animal appear numerous times will also give you more certainty that it is indeed your Power Animal. That being said, you shouldn't sit around until you notice its signs. Feel free to go about your day as usual, and let the animal come to you with the guidance you need. If your schedule allows it, you may visit the closest piece of nature to bring yourself closer to the spirit of your animal and help it appear sooner. Don't be discouraged if you aren't able to do this because your Power Animal will be able to find you even if you aren't close to nature.

If your practices involve drawing cards or any similar divination form, you can use this method to retrieve your Power Animal or at least seek some signs from it. Ask for a sign from your animal before drawing a card, and try to interpret the message you receive through the card. Depending on how specific your questions or needs are, the answer may differ. If you need an immediate resolution, the animal will most certainly appear to you soon in an unmistakable way. However, if you ask your Power Animal to accompany you on a particular path, be prepared to only encounter it in subtle signs around you.

## Following Other Animals

As mentioned before, your Power Animal will appear to you multiple times. Even if you notice an animal in times of need, one encounter cannot be considered a clear indicator that this particular animal is your Power Animal. Nevertheless, if you notice several different animals appearing simultaneously, you shouldn't deem their appearance irrelevant. If this happens under unusual circumstances, they may be trying to lead you to your true Power Animal. One of the main reasons some people believe they have multiple Power Animals is because they have encountered several different animals. Since these encounters happened when they needed the most guidance in their lives, they believe that all these animals were Power Animals. However, these animals are only transient helpers that push you in the right direction as you journey to meet your Power Animal. It's also said that Power Animals possess the spirit of many different animals, which makes it easier for them to communicate with other beings. If you ask for guidance and you have a single encounter with an animal soon after doing so, ask them about your Power Animal. Even if they aren't your guides themselves, they will send your message to your Power Animal.

**Trusting Your Instincts**

Having a lifelong affinity to a particular animal may be a clue that they are your Power Animal. If there is an animal you have been fascinated with for a long time (and you regularly drew it when you were a child or saw it in your dreams), you may have been communicating with your Power Animal all along. This can be particularly true if you have never actually seen the animal in real life - but this could mean you noticed signs of it everywhere around you. They have been preparing you subconsciously, so when it comes time for them to enter your life, you can accept them consciously. If you have such an animal in your life, your instincts tell you that you always had a friend when you needed one, even without being aware of their help. Now that you are ready to embrace the full aspect of your Power Animal, all you need to do is keep trusting your instincts. They will lead you to the animal that will teach you how to embrace their power as well as your own.

**Being Prepared to Accept Their Gifts**

You may have been aware of being accompanied by a Power Animal all your life. Or, you have just learned that you possibly have one and decided to retrieve its strength. Whichever path you are taking to meet your Power Animal, you must be prepared to accept their support through all things. The animal will not show you their support in a way you want it, but the way you need it. Albeit, each Power Animal, has its own ability. These creatures possess a higher level of spirituality and intelligence that draws strength from an entire species. This makes their gifts so valuable and unique in the sense that they are able to provide specific types of help in the exact magnitude you need. Even if you aren't aware of requiring assistance, your Power Animal will know and offer its gift to you. No matter how surprised you are about its appearance in your life, you should always accept the help that comes from your Power Animal. This will help you build a strong relationship with your animal on which you will be able to rely for the rest of your life.

**Working with Shamans**

Another way to perform a Power Animal Retrieval is to work with a Shaman and ask them to accompany you on this journey. Since they are more versed in the art of recognizing the core gift each animal brings, they will be able to help you connect with yours. They will typically do this by journeying to the Lower World and looking for your power animal on your behalf. They will ask that your Power Animal show itself to them multiple times and its message for their human spirit. This helps uncover the reasons behind it coming forward when they do. If you also accompany the Shaman on the journey to the Lower World, your retrieval will be even more successful. After all, it's you who the animal is looking to connect with, so they will be much more likely to show themselves to you than they would to the Shaman.

Your Power Animal wants to share their gift with you, and it wants to teach you how to become a better person spiritually. However, they are only able to do this if you honor the connection you have with them. Feel free to communicate with them regularly, even if you don't need them at that time. If you nurture your bond and keep it alive, your Power Animal will become an invaluable part of your life. Furthermore, the animal will always know that its help is appreciated, and it will never be tempted to leave your side.

## Chapter 5: Power Animal Magic, Tools and Crafts

Once you have discovered your Spirit Animal, the eternal question that has been at the back of your mind since you started reading this guide will come to the fore - how to use Power Animal magic? The thrill of calling your Spirit Guide and getting an answer in return is an exciting prospect in itself. However, being able to perform magical feats with your Power Animal and imbibing its strengths and attributes is an entirely different level of exhilaration altogether.

As you may already know, your Spirit Animal could be anyone, including a fellow human, for we are all inherently animals. The primary issue with having a human as a Spirit Guide is the various limitations on the corresponding Shamanic rituals. Quite a few rituals require you to take a part of the animal's physical body, like a powdered bit of skin or a piece of bone. It is important to acquire these parts ethically, like when the animal dies of natural causes or meets with an accident. You can see how difficult this task may be if you have a particular human for a Spirit Guide.

A dog is probably the easiest Power Animal to work with, especially if you own a pet. It literally guides and accompanies you in your life's journey, protects you from harm, and warns you of any impending danger. It shows you the true meaning of unconditional love. It is indeed a sad day when your dog passes away, but you can keep its spirit alive through various Shamanic rituals, for they have the ability to light up your life even in death. The same doesn't hold true if a celebrity or a mythical figure turns out to be your Spirit Animal.

That said, discovering your Power Animal is the hard part, and kudos to you if you have successfully accomplished this feat. Extracting its virtues and demystifying its magical properties is relatively easy, but don't take things lightly. Shamanic Spirit Guide magic and its associated tools and crafts can be very dangerous in the hands of the uninitiated. Even accomplished Shamans require a keen eye and should be able to delicately handle the ingredients used in the rituals.

To accentuate the seriousness of Power Animal magic, let us start with the hardest one of the lot - the animal parts ritual. It is mostly used by the Wiccan shamans and has around a thousand-year history of supporting its mysterious magic. However, for the magic to work, you will need a strong connection with your Spirit Animal, great attention to detail, and a high level of dexterity while arranging and performing the rituals.

## Animal Parts Ritual

According to Wiccan Shamanic traditions, animal parts are a powerful source of magic even when they are simply used as home decorations, personal adorations, or accessories. Donning a bear claw necklace or a hat adorned with stag antlers can often be more effective than performing a full-fledged ritual with the respective animal parts. Pick any craftable part of your Spirit Animal, like bones, hide, teeth, etc., and make a piece of ornament out of it. As long as the parts are obtained ethically, and you wear the accessory regularly, you will eventually imbibe the powers of your Spirit Animal, and it will guide you through the ups and downs of regular life.

However, to experience the full effects of the magic lent by your Power Animal, you need to perform the relevant rituals. There are two ways to gather the required animal parts - naturally discarded parts and harvesting from dead animals. Bird feathers are the easiest to acquire because loose ones often fall to the ground as they fly around. Snakes tend to shed their skin about four times every year, and deer antlers fall off during the spring season.

You can harvest any part of the animal once it is dead, either of natural causes or through an accident. Before using these parts for the ritual, you will need to purify them. Consecrate it with holy water and all the relevant Wiccan spells that you know. Only then will you be able to use them for Shamanic rituals effectively. Imbibing the animal's attributes, like strength, speed, and agility will be the most basic advantages of performing the rituals. Alternatively, you can also use the results of your rituals to divine your future path in the journey of life.

## Creating Power Animal Tools

This is where you will need your Spirit Animal to be dead before collecting its organs because no animal drops its bones naturally or sheds its tissues at will. More often than not, you will require your Power Animal's internal organs and bones to create powerful tools and crafts. However, why exactly are these tools so sought after in the world of Spirit Walking?

You may have already developed a stable connection with your Spirit Animal, or you may still struggle to establish a solid relationship. With the help of Shamanic tools, you can easily develop a bond with your Spirit Guide from scratch or greatly strengthen that already-existing connection. For example, beating drums and shaking rattles made out of animal hide accentuate your call to the wild, thus accelerating the meeting between you and your Spirit Animal. To that effect, let us start off by learning how to create a rattle.

**Making a Rawhide Rattle**

There is an easy, pretty much-standardized way of creating your very own Shamanic rattle. A complete list of the things you will need are:

- Rawhide (ideal if it is made from the skin of your Power Animal)
- A tiny piece of deerskin
- A medium-sized stick for the handle
- Artificial animal sinew
- Wool roving
- Two small pebbles (no larger than 3 mm in diameter)
- Pencil
- Piece of plywood
- Crafting tools like scissors, hammer, nails, needles, sandpaper, embroidery hook, glue, etc.

Soak the rawhide in water for around eight hours. Meanwhile, polish the wooden stick with sandpaper to make it smooth. Don't forget to thank your Spirit Guide while polishing and decorating your rattle's handle. Measure the circumference of the stick after sanding it. Once the rawhide is well-soaked and pliable, trace the outline of your desired pattern on the skin with a pencil, keeping the circumference of the handle in mind. Fold the hide along the circumference of the stick near the top, and place a tiny piece of plywood underneath, where the two ends of the hide meet. Remove the handle and punch holes into the plywood, then hammer the nails to stabilize the rawhide's shape.

Begin sewing the hide from its mouth, leaving a trail of the artificial animal sinew at each end. Feed the mouth of the hide with as much wool as it can hold so that the structure becomes nice and round. Leave this contraption out to dry in the sun for a few hours. Ensure that the rawhide has become hard enough before removing all the wool from inside with an embroidery hook. Drop the pebbles in the contraption, smear a bit of glue around the mouth, and insert the handle. Let it dry for a few minutes.

Finally, drill a minuscule hole through the hide and the inserted stick, and tie the ends of the artificial sinew through and around it to secure the rattle better. You can now start shaking your newly made rawhide rattle to the tune of your Spirit Guide's theme, thus strengthening your bond with the Shamanic spiritual realm. The rattle-based Power Animal rituals differ from tribe to tribe and region to region. Pick the song and the dance that best rouses your consciousness and spontaneously transfer it to the Lower World (Animal Spirit realm).

**Creating a Smudging Feather**

As the name suggests, a smudging feather is a special kind of feather used for smudging or cleansing a place, thing, or body. Smudging is an ancient Shamanic ritual that includes burning sacred herbs and wafting the smoke around the room using a consecrated feather.

Before you learn how to create a smudging feather, it is important to know the different kinds of feathers you can use.

- **Eagle:** Most Shamanic tribes consider the eagle to be the only living being closest to the Creator, spiritually and physically. So naturally, its feathers are considered mightily sacred for smudging. Elder Shamans aren't very picky about the type of eagle used for its feathers. Right from the mysterious golden eagle to the magnificent bald one, every eagle held an equal place in the eyes of indigenous ancients.

- **Hawk:** Shamans may not give the shawl a spiritual status equal to the eagle, but the former generally flies as high as and soars for a longer period than the King of Birds. The hawk's feathers are still considered divine for smudging, given that it flies so close to the Creator. You can often find the feather of a red-tailed hawk used by the indigenous tribes of the Americas.

- **Turkey**: The turkey is among the largest birds to roam the land and skies of Shamanic terrain. The Shamans believe that it not only keeps danger away from their settlements but also offers itself as food for them in times of famine. That is the reason why turkey feathers are sacred for the smudging ritual.

A major point to note: It is illegal in some regions to collect stray feathers of certain birds, even if you find them in a forest. Always look up the local feather laws of the area you reside in before you go out looking for an eagle feather or two. That being said, you don't need to find the feather yourself or directly pluck it from the bird to experience an effective smudging ceremony.

You can purchase a feather from a Shamanic shop in your town. Suppose you have a cordial relationship with an indigenous tribe in your vicinity. In that case, you may even be lucky enough to be given a skillfully crafted smudging feather as a gift from their chief. Alternatively, you may consider buying an artificial eagle feather from an imitation jewelry store. If you don't have access to any of the aforementioned sources, then you can always perform the smudging ritual with your dominant hand - it's acceptable in Shaman traditions, and it certainly works!

However, if you manage to get yourself that valuable bird feather, here are a few simple steps to make it suitable for the smudging ritual.

> **1.** Pick a simple wooden stick and burnish it well, first with a knife to straighten it up a bit and then with sandpaper to smooth it out.
>
> **2.** If your feather is big enough to drive smoke into the farthest corners of your room, then directly tie it to the stick with a piece of string. If not, then you may have to string a couple or three feathers together before attaching them to the stick.
>
> **3.** Wrap a long leather cord at the junction to strengthen the feather's bond with the stick and coil it around the rest of the handle for added grip.

## Casting the Bones

When you think about casting bones, your mind usually conjures the image of an old, wrinkled woman dressed in ancient Native American attire, throwing bone pieces on a termite-infested table like shooting dice at Craps. However, casting bones for Shamans is more of a fantastical art than a wild gamble. Before diving into the specifics of this art, it's better to talk about the ethics behind acquiring the bones for the purpose of Power Animal magic.

You cannot just wrench a bone out of a living animal's body. Nor are you allowed to surgically remove it. It is a crime of the highest order in Shamanic beliefs (and with local forestry law enforcement too), unnervingly barbaric and inhuman to boot! Even if you are less inclined to listen to your conscience, it's highly dangerous to your physical well-being because many animals possess fatal self-defense instincts.

Purchase your Animal Spirit's bone from a local Shamanic vendor instead. They usually harvest the bones from an already dead animal before burying or burning its corpse with the proper rituals. Additionally, if you tend to venture into your town's forest reserves, you may stumble upon a long-dead creature's bones. Collect those in your sack and head straight toward the forest department. Request the authorities to allow you to keep a bone or two. Unless the animal is an endangered species and is incredibly rare, or you have managed to find a dinosaur fossil, they may just grant your request.

Ethical rules aside, there may also be several state and regional laws against the collection of animal bones. Read through the forestry department's guidelines thoroughly before saving a bone for yourself. As George Orwell once said, Big Brother is watching you. Go for one of those imitation bones instead. They may not be equally effective, but they almost always do the trick.

Once you have finally managed to get your hands on that precious little bone, imitation or real, of your Power Animal, it's time to prepare it for casting. This is the most difficult part of the entire process, even harder than acquiring the bone. That is because there isn't really a standardized procedure that defines the right casting steps. At their core, every individual is different, and so is every animal bone.

You need to calm your mind, unclutter your thoughts, and focus your entire being on the bone that you hold in your hand and listen. Hear what it is trying to say, catch its faintest whispers, heed its complex conundrums, and attempt to untangle the fantastic enigma it conveys. Your absolute belief in your Shamanic Spirit Guide will eventually lead you to the answer you seek. You will know that you have connected with your Animal Spirit as soon as an instant jolt of magical energy courses through your veins, enlightening your soul with the right yet unique way to cast that piece of bone.

The procedure may seem vague and uncertain on the first read, but you will definitely realize its reality after going through a similar experience. Listening to what an apparently inanimate object has to say is a tough ask for many people, and even indigenous Shaman novices sometimes struggle with this task. So, don't lose hope, and keep trying until you get there.

**Of Laws and Ethics**

We have already discussed this in parts in the previous sections, but we simply cannot stress the ethical and lawful nature of Power Animal Magic enough. There was a reason why these ancient, pure Shamanic rituals were forced to don an evil, demonic mask by other religions. Most of the blame probably lies on the preachers of the other religions themselves, for they may have misconstrued the nature of those ancient practices.

Some blame may also fall into the laps of the few misinformed practitioners of the Shamanic craft. It isn't hard to twist a pure religious sentiment into a vile, chaotic aberration, and the ancestral Shamans have experienced their share of those; more than enough, some may add. There are always a few perverse individuals in every religion who tend to distort and warp the true nature of their beliefs for their own selfish gains.

As a genuine practitioner of Shamanic Power Animal tools, it is your responsibility to learn and implement the methods of the craft without violating any material, ethical, or moral rules and laws. Know that there are several places worldwide where collecting animal parts is illegal. Determine, without a shred of a doubt, that your town isn't one of those places. Law enforcement information is available freely on the internet these days, even some about the forestry department.

If Google fails you in your venture to find a detailed guideline about animal parts for your region, don't hesitate to visit the forestry office directly. Ask for said documents from the personnel at hand, and if they deny you the information, send in a formal request to the department head. If your local forestry department is efficient, you will definitely receive the required information on your doorstep within a day or two. Wait a week at most before lodging a formal complaint at the mayor's office.

As soon as the copies of local forestry laws are handed over to you, sift through the pages to locate the information about the animal parts that you require. You will often find that naturally shredded snakeskin or stag antlers will belong to the one who first noticed it. However, for the other parts, you will need to visit your local Shaman's store or a store that sells imitation items. Animal bones are especially hard to acquire unless, of course, you are connected, socially and spiritually, with your nearby indigenous tribe.

In reality, it doesn't matter where or how you get your Animal Spirit's parts, as long as the method conforms to the ethical laws of Shamanic rituals. A traditionally gifted feather or a fresh piece of shredded skin may provide the most effective results, but an imitation bone or a synthetic animal hide might be equally effective under the right circumstances. And an integral part of those circumstances is your level of belief in the Shamanic ritual that you are performing.

For instance, casting a real bone into an apparent perception of your Animal Spirit without listening to what that calcium-infused tissue is trying to convey will have no effect whatsoever on the end result of your ritual. On the other hand, performing a similar ritual with an artificial bone, complete with cleaning and consecrating the item in the right manner, but this time, having infallible belief in the ancient Shamanic customs will certainly lead you to indulge in a more intimate conversation with your Power Animal, an interaction that will eventually brighten up your path into the yet unexplored domains of the fascinating dimension of the Lower World.

# Chapter 6: Healing with Animal Medicine

This final practical chapter is dedicated to Animal Medicine, as viewed by Shamanic cultures. From here, you will learn how Animal Medicine works and the various ways you can connect with Power Animals for healing purposes. By gaining insight into several practical techniques, you will gain the ability to heal with the help of your Spirit Animal. That being said, it's important to note that if you have any mental or physical health issues, you should always consult a medical professional first about it. While this chapter could be perceived as instructions for healing your spirit, its purpose is to assist with overcoming your health concerns by empowering you from within. However, as the mind and body are so closely connected, the healing of the spirit will only yield its fruit if you take care of your body.

## Animal Medicine in Shamanic Cultures

If you have connected with your Power Animal, you have already tapped into the world of Shamanic Medicine. Welcoming this being means accepting their role as your spiritual guide, an act that in itself has powerful healing effects. In Shamanism, to heal is to release the roadblocks from your mind and dissipate all the harmful energy inside you that's getting in the way of remembering who you are and who you can be. Unfortunately, our busy world intertwined with technology often separates us from our spirits. As a result of this detachment, we often forget that we were created to remember how powerful we are. By connecting with the Spiritual Realm, you can remind yourself of your own strength. While you can use many techniques to achieve this during your Shamanic practices, your Power Animal can magnify your strength and facilitate your connection with the Spirits. This will help you heal your scars from within by overcoming your ego, but it will also become a powerful tool in practicing Shamanic Medicine.

In Shamanic cultures, everything is medicine because everything has a spirit. Practicing Shamanic Medicine means choosing the path of inner power and combining it with nature's power. By doing this, you can become more powerful both in spirit and body and share this power through healing medicine. When you harness the power of a natural element, this becomes your ally, your inner healer. Sharing your healing power with your Spirit Animal makes you feel more grounded and capable of nurturing anyone in need. In addition, each Power Animal has their own medicine. Some animals specialize in carrying divine messages, while others are excellent at spiritual cleansing. When you are getting to know your Power Animal, it will communicate its gift to you to understand how you may rely on its help in the future.

## How Animal Medicine Works

Animal Medicine is an ancient practice reborn in the spiritual rituals of Shamanism. It connects the spirit of Shamans and Shamanic practitioners with the spirit of their Power Animals through revelation, Shamanic journeying, ceremonies, rituals, or meditation. According to Shamanic traditions, animals are our guides both in this world and in the next one. Besides protecting your spirit, your Power Animal will help you acquire ancient wisdom and share the knowledge with others. By creating a spiritual bridge and inviting your Power Animal to cohabit with you, you will also allow its spirit to impart wisdom, further enriching your practice.

Practitioners of the Ancient Shamanic beliefs prepared themselves for a hunt, battle, or any future action that required protection by completing a ceremony during which they connected with the spirit of an animal and asked it to give its life for their tribe. However, unlike in many other cultures, the sacrificed animal wasn't discarded after completing the ritual. Instead of letting it go to waste, they used every part of it for sustenance, protection, and shelter.

The ancestors acknowledged that the cycle of life contained both death and life. They also expressed their gratitude for Nature's help in sustaining them by incorporating themselves into the natural ecosystem. By acknowledging the harmony between them and their food source, they could express their appreciation on a much higher level. Not only was the sacrificed animal used for sustenance, but its spirit was also acknowledged as a guide, and its life was immortalized. The animal was celebrated as part of their tribe's totem - a tradition passed down through generations in tales, incorporating it into the tribe's oral history.

In modern-day Shamanism, we acknowledge the gift of our Power Animals. By doing so, we also celebrate their ancestors who gave their lives so we could survive. This will assure that when called on, your Power Animal can impart the ancient wisdom they carry so they can assist your Shamanic journeys toward self-healing. It also makes the Power Animal's spirit more comfortable to work with you without boundaries or limitations, allowing it to join you anytime you need them. By incorporating ancient knowledge into the Physical Realm, Animal Medicine creates a medium to invite natural power into your practice.

## Connecting with Power Animals for Healing

Your Power Animal will let you know when and how it wants to work with you. It will usually do this by appearing multiple times - either in physical form or in any other representation of itself. Whether its spirit visits you in your dreams or when you are awake, you will definitely feel its pull. When this happens, you must draw your Power Animal closer and form an even greater bond with them. Putting up symbols of your Spirit Animal around your home or altar or inviting it to your morning rituals is a great way to honor them. You can also compliment the animal and express your gratitude for its presence in your life. After that, you can proceed with telling them how they can help you. Don't forget to thank them for their assistance in advance.

Once you learn the basics of communicating with your Spirit Animal, you will be able to understand the messages it carries and interpret their meanings. This will give you an insight into proceeding with your actions. Whenever you feel the need to ask for their guidance in healing, seek out a place where you can calm your spirit. After using meditation to become relaxed, reach out to your Power Animal and make your inquiry concerning healing. The animal will appear in your mind's eye and guide you to the right path. Listen carefully to its message and watch everything it does as well. Remember, Power Animals often communicate through actions rather than words. Once it has finished conveying the spiritual message, the animal will disappear, and you can return to the Physical Realm. Write down everything you saw and heard, so you will remember the message when it's time to take action.

You can send your Spirit Animal off to do hard work of sorting out your emotions and taking off the load on your shoulders. This way, you will be able to complete all your daily tasks smoothly and efficiently, leading you closer to your personal goals. If you practice Shamanic Medicine, you can also invite your Power Animal into your healing work to guide you or anyone else that needs healing. When doing so, remember that the spirits only work in sacred ways. They can be a great tool to harness natural healing power but will only help you find your flow if you honor them in your everyday life. Doing this will remind you of your own inner strength. However, your work with them will also make sure you remember you are not alone in this Universe.

## Factors That May Affect Your Practice

When you embark on your Shamanic journeys, you will also meet other creatures. Each of them has its own gift they can impart to you and a specific message you can use during your healing practices. Your Power Animal can help you communicate with the spirit of these creatures and convey their messages if necessary. With this knowledge, you will have a greater understanding of the natural forces, which will help you determine the proper healing method for each individual.

As a Shamanic practitioner, you must acknowledge that the help you get from your Power Animal is only part of achieving the wholeness of any healing ritual. If you weren't able to gather your inner power and overcome your own issues, you wouldn't be able to help anyone. So, the first step in your journey to Animal Medicine is to let your Power Animal heal you. Once you are free of any psychological and environmental roadblocks, you will be ready to share your powers. The problem is, you may not even be aware of your problems until they become too evident - and this is true for other people as well. Going on a Shamanic journey with your Power Animal can lead you to become more acquainted with your spirit. This will help you counsel others in similar matters in the future.

The second factor that may affect your practice is modern medicine. The same your hands are guided by the spirits, also are the hands of a modern medical practitioner. For this reason, their work must be honored for its value. When envisioning your approach to healing, you must consider the protocols prescribed by modern medicine as well. Your success in this endeavor depends on your experience in the different types of Shamanic healing techniques. You must learn to listen to your Power Animal, for it will guide you in the direction you need to go.

## Healing Techniques You Can Use
### Becoming Your Own Healer
To heal others, first you will need to make sure you are healthy enough to harness all the powers that the Spirits may provide you. When you are making inquiries on behalf of others, the Spirits will test you, and if you fail their test, you won't be able to help anyone. So, before you embark on the journey to find the medicine for someone else, you must cleanse yourself. You can do this through meditation, prayers, trance, different rituals, dance, or whichever practice frees your mind and body from negative energy. Only when your mind is open will you be able to travel to the Spiritual Realm and seek insight or guidance with your healing.

## Combining Powers

You will find that your healing is most effective when you are able to work in tandem with the spirit of your Power Animal or the essence of any other creature or human being. Not only will your medicine change as you gain experience and wisdom, but the spirits are all subjected to change as well. So, for your medicine to work, you should consider the needs of all the souls surrounding the particular condition you are trying to remedy. In return, you will forge a connection with all these spirits, and you may be able to call upon them should you require their help in the future. Since all of them have their own specialty, you will have many allies you can employ in various areas of your life, not just for healing.

## Asking for Assistance

While your Power Animal may choose to connect with you, they won't intrude upon your spirit unless you require their assistance. Once you understand how they can help you with your medicine, you will know when you can call them for help. You will be able to blend their healing abilities with yours and enhance your natural power. Using the same technique of relaxation you do when you are getting to know your Power Animal, seek out its spirit and ask if you can borrow it. As long as you honor your bond with them, Power Animals are usually happy to be of assistance.

## Creating a Medicine Wheel

The Medicine Wheel is a notable symbol of balance and harmonious connections in nature. It's also a medium through which you can learn and enrich your Shamanic healing practices. You can create it with different colors and animal spirits - and use it for various healing rituals and Shamanic journeys. Being a newcomer in the world of Shamanic healing, you might find the concept of the Medicine Wheel challenging to comprehend - much less creating one on your own. However, you must understand that the Medicine Wheel actually represents the circle of life - your life and the life of every creature around you. Therefore, you must see to these tasks based on your experience and the teaching you receive from your Power Animal.

You can begin by creating the center of the Medicine Wheel and the most valuable to you in it. Whether it's pure hearth, truth, the Great Spirit, or the Creator, the choice is yours. But remember that everything originates from the center and comes together at its core, so you must choose it wisely. You may also add your name to the center. After all, even though you may rely on other spirits for guidance, it will be up to you to use your powers wisely. Placing your name in the center will also reiterate the belief that in order to help others, you must take time for regular self-care as well - because if you don't, the well won't either.

Divide the inside of the circle into four quadrants - these will be your four directions. Name them in a clockwise direction, following the path of the Sun from the time it rises to the time it sets. Your next step will be to place the areas of your life in each quadrant. Begin with putting the physical aspect in the east. This direction is the first one in the Sun's path, and it also represents the beginning of your physical life on this planet. Continue with placing your mental area in the south quadrant, signifying the time in your life when you begin to use and develop your mind. Move onto the west with your emotions, then finish the circle with your spirituality in the north area.

Now it's time to find the animals that best represent the four directions and add them to the circle. The Sun in the east is often associated with the eagle, and this sacred animal is said to carry many spiritual messages. Therefore, if you want to receive beneficial advice through the wheel, you must place the eagle in the east quadrant. This knowledge can particularly come in handy if you are confronted with a serious medical issue you need spiritual guidance to resolve. The eagle will send you a powerful message which will enlighten you to find the best healing method.

Following the Sun's direction, you arrive in the south quadrant, representing the time most offerings are made. In ancient times, the animal used for these offerings was the buffalo - because it provided the most supplies for sustenance and shelter. For this reason, it was, and still is, the most honored one in the Shamanic practices. By putting the buffalo in the south, you will continue this tradition of honoring its spirit. And if you make an offering of your own using the Medicine Wheel, you can count on its blessings. Since this animal is also a strong protector by nature, it will be the most useful to you for warding off diseases and injuries.

The west represents your emotional state, which must be balanced to be able to practice Shamanic Medicine. The animal that can help you maintain your balance is the bear. Similar to you, this animal stands firmly on two legs and is considered to wield enormous spiritual power. By adding the bear onto the west quadrant of the Medicine Wheel, you will always be able to draw enough strength for your practice. Whether you need to heal yourself or someone else in your life, you can call upon the spirit of the bear and all its ancestors to supply you with all the power you need.

When you arrive in the north quadrant, you will reach your spirituality. This part of the Medicine Wheel is often used to gather spiritual wisdom you may lack to find the rich approach in your healing practice. The wolf is considered to be one of the most astute animals on the planet, and therefore, you will make great use of it in your north quadrant. This four-legged animal is able to overcome many difficulties in its life and survive even the harshest conditions in this world. It also travels in packs, so it may teach you how to connect with your community. All these qualities are multiplied in all the ancestral wolf spirits you can reach through your Medicine Wheel.

A Medicine Wheel can teach you several important lessons. When you look at the different animals represented in your circle, you think of balance and harmony that needs to exist between them. You will start to see that if all these creatures can work together and provide you with the necessary guidance, you could also balance your life by aiming to work with all the spirits around you. Another teaching in the Medicine Wheel is that you have *choices.* You can choose how you live your life and how to use your gifts. The way you decide to use the medicine you receive from the four animals will be your choice. But remember, the spirits will only help you if you intend to use their gifts positively.

The illustrations used to explain the combined power of the circle can help you become a better healer. By applying the Medicine Wheel in a way that improves your emotional well-being first, you will get to a healthy mental, spiritual, and physical state. Then you will be able to use the circle positively, and, in turn, it will reward you with many blessings in life. Not only will this guide you with your Shamanic practices and journeys, but it will also help you gather all the strength and wisdom you can throughout your life.

# PART THREE: Animal Spirit Guide List and Meanings

Understanding the presence of Spirit Animals and guides isn't enough. You need to learn about the different Spirit Animals – and what each of them represents – to understand the message the universe is trying to give you. Some cultures believe that when you cross paths with a particular animal, it's the universe's way of trying to tell you something. Whether it's a lesson to be taught or much-needed guidance in a time of desperation, the animals around you symbolize and mean something. This list will explore the symbolism behind each Spirit Animal you could come across and what that could mean to you during your spiritual journey. All you need to do is stop and listen to those messages, and they will make a difference in your life.

Moreover, as a Power or Spirit Animal, each of these unique beasts mirrors your personality traits that you might not even fully understand yet. As you know by now, each of us has a spirit or power animal defined by several factors, and you need to fully understand yours. The more you learn about the traits of your spirit animal, the more you can learn about yourself and unlock your full potential. Most importantly, though, understanding the traits of your spirit animal helps you come to terms with your own traits and accept the parts of your personality that you may have struggled with in the past at some point or the other.

## 1. Butterfly

In terms of symbolism, butterflies have always been associated with significant transformation or a large and profound change that you are about to undergo. Some civilizations also believed that butterflies are associated with the cycle of death and rebirth, which can be interpreted as a part of yourself slowly disappearing and giving way to a new version. Another way to consider an encounter with a butterfly is how they resemble lightness of being and constant motion. Perhaps the encounter with a butterfly is a reminder that you should always be moving forward in life and in a constant state of motion. Colorful and joyful creatures as they are, perhaps the encounter is the universe's way of telling you to get up, dance, and have some fun!

**As a Guide**: As an Animal Spirit Guide, the butterfly will come into your life when you are experiencing a life-changing transformation. It will help you embrace those changes and accept them wholeheartedly with peace and serenity rather than frustration and contempt. Change isn't always easy, and a butterfly spirit guide will help make the transition a little bit smoother. It will ground you and preserve your energy as you undergo the change while also helping you maintain the belief that this change is for the greater good.

**As a Spirit Animal**: Those with butterflies as spirit animals are often capable of embracing change with grace and dignity, content with the rewards of the journey itself rather than a particular outcome. They have faith and almost always come out with life-changing transformations as better people with a more defined purpose. Butterflies as spirit animals also symbolize harmony and a connection to the earth, meaning people with this spirit animal are most likely to care deeply for the environment and do whatever they can to help it.

## 2. Cat

Cats symbolize balance and communication. They're also expressive of mystery, magic, and curiosity. The balance meant here is often between opposites — light and dark, rest and action, and so on. Cats are associated with the unknown mysteries that lie in the darkness since they are curious creatures by nature who often seek out knowledge and satisfaction of that curiosity. A lot of cultures believe that cats have a strong connection to the spirit world and often symbolize a connection between our world and the spirit world. This may be because cats are more active at night and can see in the dark, which is also why they were often associated with witchcraft and dark magic.

**As a Guide:** When you encounter a cat, this might mean that someone out there or something is trying to give you a message that might just be from beyond the veil. You need to listen and communicate with the cat to try and get the message that might just make a significant difference in your life. Cats as spirit guides may be a sign that you need more balance in your life, especially between independence and together-time with your loved ones. In simpler terms, when you encounter a cat as a spirit guide, particularly at times when you feel stuck and stagnant, this may be the time to explore the unknown and try new things. Come out of your comfort zone and explore new horizons. Your cat spirit guide will help you understand that you have it in you to create the things you want and that you have the skills and ability to succeed.

**As a Spirit Animal:** People with cats as spirit animals are naturally curious and creative. If a cat is your spirit animal, you are also independent and capable of doing things without relying on anyone. There's also an air of mystery surrounding you, and you are private and very selective about those who you let into your inner circle. You never succumb to peer pressure, and you do what you want rather than what others want you to do.

### 3. Spider

Much like cats, spiders are also mysterious creatures associated with creativity, wisdom, and growth. The spider weaves and creates destiny paths, teaching us how to walk them with confidence and care so that we may trust the process. Spiders are a reminder that we can create the life that we want and weave its webs like a spider. These creatures are extremely patient as they have to be to build the kind of creations that they do, and we can learn a lot from spiders in terms of waiting for good things to happen without rushing them. In some cultures, spiders are also associated with feminine energy.

**As a Guide**: A spider will guide you to tap into your creative side and help you embrace your ideas so you can act upon them. With a spider as your spirit guide, you won't doubt your creativity and second-guess your ideas and dreams. One thing to learn from a spider guide is that you do not have to settle. If your life, in its current form, doesn't suit you or make you happy, then it's time to weave a new one that better suits your hopes and dreams.

**As a Spirit Animal:** If a spider is your spirit animal, you are a creator, blessed with creativity and intellect and the patience to wait to see the fruit of your labor. You are confident and not afraid of exploring the unknown. You are also capable of achieving the balance between the male and female aspects of your personality and the past and future. People with spider spirit animals are doers who don't hesitate to take action, and they are excellent decision-makers who rarely make the wrong choice, driven by the spider's ability to observe and patiently strike when it finds the right opportunity.

## 4. Ant

There are few creatures as diligent as ants, known for their patience and loyalty. If an ant manifests before you, it may be a message that you need to work with diligence and conviction to pursue your goals in life and turn your dreams into reality. Ants are as tenacious as any other spirit animal, and they don't stop until they get what they want, without caring about their small size that might otherwise be a disadvantage. They have tremendous willpower to see them through the most difficult challenges and obstacles.

**As a Guide**: Ants may act as a spirit guide to help you find the strength to move past a difficult time in your life or find the courage needed to get the results that you have worked hard for. An ant will remind you that good things come after hard work and time. As your spirit guide, they may also remind you to focus on your role as a cog in a greater machine, leveraging your natural abilities to master a specialty. Ants also help you figure out how every part of your life fits in the greater picture, whether that's work, family, or your personal interests.

**As a Spirit Animal:** If an ant is your spirit animal, you are loyal to a fault and would go to great lengths to help and be there for the people that you care about. You are also an honest person who's not conceited, which is shown in how dedicated and diligent you are not just in your work but also as an active member of the community. You are also persistent, and you never give up. You are a planner, and with your dedication, you act as the architect of your life, overseeing the smallest of details that can contribute to your happiness and success.

## 5. Crow

Despite negative connotations in some minds, crows are fearless creatures associated with magic, wisdom, and transformation. Crows are symbols of change, and when one enters your life, it might mean that something good is about to happen — probably what you've been working for. One significant feature associated with crows is insight and their high intuition and perspective, as they are creatures with great vision. Crows are magical creatures with a mystical connection to life and its secrets. Crows may also be a sign that you are overworking, and you need to take a moment to assess your priorities rather than spreading yourself too thin.

**As a Guide:** A crow in your life may be a warning that you need to be mindful and careful of appearances that could deceive you. It will help you develop foresight so you can see beyond the obvious and see through people's ill intentions. A crow spirit guide will invite mystery and magic in your life, blessing you with enhanced awareness and higher intuition to help you see the magic in everything. A crow is also a great spirit guide to invoke when you need help facing a challenge or a major obstacle in your life, as it's a creature with great determination.

**As a Spirit Animal:** Crow people have personal integrity and are honest. They're straight shooters who don't beat around the bush while still being considerate enough not to hurt others with their words or actions. They're mindful of what they say and do, but at the same time, they do what they preach. People with a crow spirit animal can easily go through life's great changes with ease and without exerting themselves. They focus on the now rather than what might have been or the future.

## 6. Alligator

Alligators are another spirit animal associated with creativity and wisdom, but not the kind of wisdom you'd find in a poet or a shaman. Alligators are more associated with raw, primal energy and unbridled creative prowess. It's a keeper of time and a protector of knowledge. It's a reminder that we need to seek knowledge and try to embrace wisdom and new experiences that could teach us and enrich our lives. An alligator could also mean that you need to shake things up and move forward with your life rather than letting it remain stagnant. Alligators are linked to retribution and hostility in the face of aggression, which could inspire you not to accept insults and other people's needless aggression in life.

**As a Guide**: An alligator spirit guide can appear when you need the courage to accept new changes in your life and embrace what this growth can mean for your journey. It will help you find the time and desire to ingest the changes and integrate them into your life while maintaining a sense of balance during this transition. Alligators are efficient creatures who get the job done with minimal effort, which can be what you need right now, something your spirit guide will help you with.

**As a Spirit Animal:** You're brave and more confident with an alligator as your spirit animal. You don't fear change, no matter how uncomfortable it may be, because you know you will find the wisdom to accept things you cannot change. You can bring harmony to your life without waiting for certain events or people to help you find peace. You're authentic, and you help others be authentic around you because you accept them for who they are rather than who you want them to be. You are an anchor that helps people remain calm and find peace even in the midst of chaos. In other words, you're a healer.

## 7. Owl

The owl is one of the wisest spirit animals, and it is associated with the mysteries of the world, secret-keeping, and protection. It's also one of the rarer spirit animals, so if you come across one, it's a good sign, contrary to popular belief, and a message from the universe. Owls are capable of seeing beyond façades and can detect deceit, so they can help you see beyond illusion and deception. Owls are still and enjoy the serenity, indicating that you need to take a step back and look at your life to assess how it's going.

**As a Guide:** An owl spirit guide may enter your life when you need wisdom the most, probably when you are about to make a major decision or explore the unknown. It can guide you as you embark on this journey to explore life's magic. The owl will help you open your eyes and see beyond the obvious so you can make the right choices and have no fear of what is to come. An owl can also help you find the wisdom to look inward and hear your inner voice as it tells you to let go of the things and people you no longer need.

**As a Spirit Animal**: If the owl is your spirit animal, you are blessed with strong intuition that helps you see through people's barriers and lies, and you are wise enough to know the motives behind them. You are a "night owl," pun intended, who likes to work at night rather than in the morning, and that's when you are at your peak. This is why people who have owls for spirit animals have no fear of darkness or the occult, and many of them dabble in magic — some are even blessed with the gift of prophecy and clairvoyance. You know how to keep a secret and, more importantly, how to get one out of people.

## 8. Bee

Bees are associated with productivity and tenacity. They are creators and innovators that play an important role in our lives, both symbolic and physical. Bees are symbols of not just hard work and success but also communication, love, and wisdom. Bees have also often featured in myth and legend as purifiers of the soul and givers of strength and courage. They nurture harmony among people and accomplish a lot despite their small stature.

**As a Guide:** A bee will appear as a spirit guide in your life when you are in need of discipline and productivity. It will help you become more decisive and get your life in order so you can fulfill your potential. With a bee as your spirit guide, you won't miss as many opportunities due to indecisiveness and the inability to act. The bee will remind you that hard work does bear fruit, and you can accomplish the things that you want if you just keep working at it. The bee will help you become involved in collaborative efforts to build a community and a social order that brings good to all.

**As a Spirit Animal:** People with bees as spirit animals have the ability to work independently and can also work within a group, just like a bee. They understand the importance of forging bonds with others for the wellbeing of all, and they are social people who work and live harmoniously with their peers. They make great friends, and they're the kind of people that others feel drawn to. Moreover, if a bee is your spirit animal, you can achieve the impossible through hard work and dedication, and you know what you want in life. You have a laser focus, and you shine when working with others. You live to serve and benefit others, and in turn, you get satisfaction and fulfillment.

### 9. Hawk

The hawk is a formidable creature with a powerful vision and endless courage. It symbolizes self-awareness and higher truths, which is why it has been revered as a spirit guide across many civilizations since the time of ancient Egyptians. Due to its ability to spot things from a higher point, hawks also represent intuition and wisdom — the ability to see the big picture and not dwell on the finer details that add nothing to the grand narrative. If a hawk enters your life, you need to pay attention because you are being given a message that you should be mindful of.

**As a Guide:** Hawks represent an ability that all humans could stand to learn and gain from seeing meaning and value in the most mundane experiences. When a hawk acts as your spirit guide, it will help you break free of the shackles of your own thoughts and limitations so you can see the bigger picture and gain a higher perspective. This will help you grow as a person and find the wisdom to drive your life forward. You will also gain the focus often attributed to hawks and the mental clarity to take the right action.

**As a Spirit Animal:** Hawks are noble and proud creatures that bestow these qualities upon people for whom they act as spirit animals. If you're one of those lucky few, you're goal-oriented, and nothing can distract you from doing the things you set out to do. You're brave and do not fear the unknown, blessed with the ability to soar to new heights without your mind's limitations slowing you down. People with hawks as spirit animals are leaders that others look up to, and they can influence others and are almost always the ones that take the initiative. Perhaps your most important quality is your ability to be optimistic and see a better future. In a way, you see what others cannot.

## 10. Armadillo

Armadillos are sensitive creatures with a shy nature. They are calm and isolated, but they nonetheless understand the need for connection. The importance of the armadillo's symbolism is that it helps you remember that it's ok to put yourself out there and get hurt because living isn't about protecting your heart and sparing yourself from feeling. It's about trying and making the right choices, which you can only make if you let go. Armadillos are associated with protection and will help you become aware of how you can protect your physical self.

**As a Guide**: Armadillos will give you the inspiration to use the right tools for the job so you can remain safe. As your spiritual guide, the armadillo will give you the clarity to avoid doing things that may end up hurting your body. Armadillos symbolize instincts as well, which is important as it will show you how to move forward while using your instincts to minimize hurt and suffering if you fail. The armadillo will guide you through planning ahead and thinking of the risks without dwelling too much on potential outcomes, which can be debilitating.

**As a Spirit Animal**: People with armadillos as spirit animals are fortunate because they truly understand one invaluable lesson, and that is that there are dangers and pain out there, but you can't let it stop you from experiencing new things and living your life to the fullest. They're well prepared, which helps them go out there and enjoy themselves. Despite this, people with this spirit animal can be conservative and tend to shield themselves from emotional pain at first, but once they get past their fears, they are steadfast in their love and loyalty.

## 11. Eagle

Like hawks, eagles are goal-oriented and have a powerful ability to focus on their targets. Eagles are powerful and can reach heights that few other birds can, making them excellent motivators and inspiring spirit animals to have in your life. It can help you see things from a wider perspective and focus on the big picture. An eagle's presence in your life is possibly a message that you need to pay attention to your inner voice and look inward so you can connect to your spiritual path. Follow your heart's desires and let them point you in the right direction.

**As a Guide**: The eagle will manifest as your spirit guide in times when you are in desperate need of guidance and affirmation. It will help set you on the right path so you can access opportunities that you could have never dreamed of before. The eagle spirit guide will help you stay grounded, too, as they are one of the most grounded creatures with a strong connection to the Earth. It will give you the courage and strength to overcome adversity in your life.

**As a Spirit Animal:** If the eagle is your spirit animal, you're strong and brave, yet, you carry yourself with lightness, just like the eagle is the symbol of air. You can walk steadily on earth, but you can also soar to new heights and achieve great things. You understand the importance of inner growth, and you strive to become a better version of yourself every day rather than comparing yourself to others. You are successful, and you can influence people with great leadership skills. However, you also understand the importance of balance and keeping that eagle strength within you at bay so it doesn't alienate people.

## 12. Grasshopper

Grasshoppers are a sign from the universe that you need to have confidence and take a leap of faith, trusting that things will work out for you. These small creatures have often been associated with good fate and progressions, not to mention innovation and wealth. Having one in your life is a good sign that you're doing all the right things, and all you need to do is have faith to move forward rather than dwelling on your fears and concerns.

**As a Guide:** The grasshopper will appear as your spirit guide when you need it the most in times of hesitation before taking a major decision. This can be moving on from an unhealthy relationship, taking a career step, moving away from a location, or even making a change within yourself to become a better person. The grasshopper will help you take that leap of faith and have the courage to see things through. A grasshopper spirit guide will remind you that you have the wisdom needed to move forward in your life. You are where you need to be, and it's time to move forward.

**As a Spirit Animal**: You're innovative and have confidence in your own intellect and wisdom. A grasshopper for a spirit animal means you're constantly moving forward, and you never miss an opportunity to become a better version of yourself or achieve success. Your instincts are sharp, and you trust them, which often brings you good fortune. You're also a giver who likes helping others, and it brings you joy and satisfaction.

## 13. Dolphin

Dolphins are majestic creatures that we all love, and they convey significant symbolism as spirit animals that you need to understand in case you encounter one. Dolphins symbolize balance and harmony. If one enters your life, it may be a sign that you need to strike a balance between work, family, and fun. It's a reminder to stop being so serious and go have some fun.

**As a Guide:** Dolphins are associated with peace and harmony, so when one enters your life as a guide, it could be a sign that you need to relax and unwind for a bit. A dolphin's gentle nature is a constant reminder for us to be helpful and cooperate with others, just like dolphins coexist with other species, including humans. As a spirit guide, it will help you attain the mental clarity to find peace in your relationships. It will show you the importance of practicing love for others around you and how it can make your life significantly better. With a dolphin spirit guide, you will focus more on the similarities between you and others rather than the differences.

**As a Spirit Animal:** People with dolphins as spirit animals are lively and fun to be around. You're the person within your circles that people call if they want to spend a care-free night. Like dolphins, you always see the good in people, which is why you are liked by most. You're also intelligent and a giver with a generous spirit. Moreover, as dolphins are protective, so are you, and you protect those you care about and offer guidance in any way you can.

## 14. Bear

Bears are animals they should fear for many people, but there is much more to them than brute power and ferocity. Bears symbolize understanding and introspection. When one enters your life, it's the universe's way of telling you that you need to look inward and explore your depth so you can get a better understanding of who you are and where your path is taking you.

**As a Guide:** Bears are powerful guides that can help you achieve spiritual and physical healing after an emotional trauma or an accident. They have a great connection to the earth, and as your spirit guide, they can help you remain grounded and calm in the face of adversity. A bear spirit guide will also remind you of your own free will and that you have the luxury of making your own choices and following your path. It will give you the confidence to embark on your journey without constantly looking back. The bear will teach you to self-reflect so you can heal from past traumas and move forward in life.

**As a Spirit Animal**: A bear for your spirit animal means that you're strong and brave. You don't let people walk over you, and you command respect wherever you go, whether it's your personal or professional life. You're confident in who you are, and you know what you want in life. You enjoy your own company, and you don't mind solitude. In fact, you find comfort and harmony in it.

### 15. Camel

Camels are associated with endurance and perseverance. If it appears in your life, it's a sign that you are on the right path and doing the right things. Take it as the universe telling you to keep doing what you're doing, and you'll find value and meaning along the way. One other way to observe the camel's symbolism is that you need to find a safe space where you can recharge your energy and find the time to nurture yourself.

**As a Guide:** The camel will enter your life as a spirit guide when you need to find the balance between work, relations, and self-love. It will help you find that space and time and headspace so you can recharge and keep walking your path. The camel will inspire you to keep moving forward and give you confidence that you will soon reap the fruits of your labor. With a camel as your spirit guide, you will find gratitude and happiness in what you have achieved, reflecting your mental well-being.

**As a Spirit Animal**: If your spirit animal is the camel, you are excellent at managing your resources, and you can stretch them for a long time, more than most people. You have an excellent work ethic, and you're committed, which reflects positively on your professional life and makes you the person that people rely on. You're self-sufficient and have strong willpower that helps you accomplish whatever you set your mind to. You're also trustworthy and kind. Last, but not least, much like the camel, you're highly adaptable to sudden changes, and you can handle extreme conditions better than most.

### 16. Deer

Deer carry a message of self-love and compassion. It symbolizes the notion that you have to forgive yourself for your past mistakes and lessen the severity of your self-criticism. They are majestic and graceful animals that represent kindness and love. The deer is a reminder to be yourself and to keep walking your path with grace and determination because good things will come if you do. Deer also symbolize generosity and the willingness to give to others, whether by helping them discover their unique qualities or using your own qualities to support them.

**As a Guide:** When you encounter a deer spirit guide, it's an important reminder that you need to be gentle with your approach to life's adversities. You cannot force change, whether on others or yourself, but you should rather tactically approach it. Deer also symbolize the importance of keeping one's innocence and purity despite all the horrors of the world so we can help others and ourselves along the journey.

**As a Spirit Animal**: Those with deer spirit animals are among the lucky few who can balance kindness with determination. They can assert themselves and stand their ground without being too crass or inconsiderate. They realize that just because they're gentle and kind doesn't mean they are defenseless, and they don't let others abuse that side of them. They see kindness in people, and they are artistic and sensitive by nature.

## 17. Horse

Horses have always been synonymous with freedom and the ability to control your destiny. It symbolizes the fact that you have it in you to change whatever you want in your life and that man is in charge of his destiny. The horse bestows a sense of adventure on us and the feeling that we are mobile, and nothing can stop us from living our lives to the fullest. It's a powerful animal with a relentless driving force that can supply people with motivation and inspiration to do what they want.

**As a Guide**: In times of despair and stagnation, the horse will appear as a spirit guide to show you that you are not forced to endure any conditions that stifle you. It will remind you of how wild and free your spirit can be if you just let go and embrace that side of yourself. The horse will also show you that you can achieve true power and freedom by showing compassion and care. It will help you share these values with others since this is what true wisdom means, and in wisdom lies great power to control our fates.

**As a Spirit Guide:** If a horse is your spirit animal, you are a wild spirit who doesn't fear the unknown and constantly embarks on new journeys. Like the horse, you ride in new directions and explore the horizon, not just to discover the unknown but also to learn about your own power and limitations. Nothing stops you in life, and whatever obstacles you come across, you're confident that you can overcome them and come out a stronger person with a new passion for liberty. You express yourself freely in life and speak your mind, but you are not rude, despite your assertiveness.

## 18. Lion

The lion is one of the most feared animals in the wild with a relentless fight in it, conquering one challenge after the other. It's a symbol of courage and strength, an authority figure, and a natural leader that often appears in folk tales like the one all animals look up to. On the other hand, lions also symbolize simplicity of sorts and remind us not to complicate things. Just focus on the essentials and relax. It prompts you to strike a balance between the different aspects of your life so you can find some solace and peace of mind.

**As a Guide:** When the lion enters your life as a spirit guide, it might be time for you to step up and assume responsibility or take charge and lead your community to greater things. It will help you understand the nobler and fiercer parts of yourself, which can help you reach new heights in life and succeed. At times, it represents fear or anger, feelings that are difficult to control and tame, just like the lion. As your spirit guide, it will help you become aware of those feelings and acknowledge them so you can find a way to deal with them.

**As a Spirit Animal**: If your spirit animal is a lion, you're very independent, and you value your freedom above all. You are untamable, but you are not dangerously wild as to spiral out of control. You're confident and feel at ease when you are in charge because you're born to be a leader. You can influence others and motivate them to become better versions of themselves. You're also creative and smart, though you don't need to show it or brag about it. Despite your natural ferocity, you're quiet and wise enough to know that you don't need to always show that side of you. You're also very loyal and would do anything to help those you love, and you'll defend them against anyone and anything.

## 19. Snake

Snakes have raw, primal energy and a strong connection to nature and the earth. In some ancient civilizations, snakes were a powerful symbol representing the source of life. The most common thing snakes are associated with is transformation and the advent of change. Like snakes, it might be the time to shed your old skin — in this case, emotions, habits, or unhealthy patterns — so you can transform into a better version of yourself. Snakes enter your life when it's time for change to remind you that you're the driving force behind that change, and it can be as you wish it to be. It could also mean that a healing opportunity looms on the horizon, and you'll be able to move past a certain painful experience.

**As a Guide:** On the verge of a major change in your life, the snake spirit guide will help you find the confidence and serenity needed to walk through that door. It will guide you through that transition and remind you that you are not alone. It will help you clear your intentions and gain a sense of direction of where you're going, in a way, driving you to understand that the changes are safe, and they will make your life better, so you don't have to be afraid. Another way the snake spirit guide will help you is it will remind you of the importance of connecting with yourself and being mindful of your surroundings and how they affect your wellbeing.

**As a Spirit Animal**: With a snake as your spirit animal, you'll have rare healing abilities that can help you move on from traumas faster than others. Your energy is balanced by virtue of the snake's primal energy. You're also quite charming, and people love to hear you talk, drawn to your intensity and ability to see through them. An air of mystery surrounds you, bolstered by your confidence and charisma, making it easy for you to engage people in lively conversation and also escape from boring ones with ease and grace.

## 20. Wolf

Wolves are protective and loyal, but they're also fierce and intelligent. They're one of the most dominant animals in the animal realm and represent intuition, tribal values, willpower, and freedom. They symbolize endurance and unwavering loyalty to their pack, despite often appearing as loners. Wolves bring a special intelligence as spirit animals, and they bestow a lust for freedom. They prompt us to connect with and trust our instincts because that is how we move forward in life.

**As a Guide:** Wolves appear as spirit guides when you need help in overcoming attempts to stifle your creativity and freedom, and it can snap you out of feelings of loneliness and self-pity. These beasts are rarely domesticated, which can signify that you need to express your true self more freely without fearing how others might view you. The wolf guide will remind you of your inner strength and stamina, not to mention the order of things and how you can find harmony in balance. Wolves also embody freedom, and you can think of it as a sign that you need to let go and be free.

**As a Spirit Animal:** If your spirit animal is a wolf, you develop strong connections and bonds with a few select people, and you are fiercely loyal to those that you care about, despite often preferring solitude. You like to explore new things, and you enjoy your time alone as much as you enjoy hanging out with those in your innermost circle. Despite your natural prowess, you prefer diplomacy and tact over picking fights and being troublesome, not out of weakness but wisdom that helps you realize that fighting isn't always the answer.

## 21. Pig

Pigs help us understand that we are enough; we have everything it takes to grow and move forward in life. If things aren't working for you, make a change. Don't be content with just going through the motions every day without any satisfaction or joy. Having a pig in your life may also mean that you are not surrounding yourself with the right people for your growth, so you might need to end some toxic relationships and keep only positive ones that enrich your life and improve your mental health.

**As a Guide:** The pig guide will come into your life to remind you that you shouldn't care too much about what other people think, and it's time for you to live your life however you want. It symbolizes not worrying about other people's views on our lives. It will help you overcome any self-doubt and limiting beliefs to succeed and do the things you want to do. The pig will also help you find focus and mental clarity to work on achieving your goals.

**As a Spirit Animal:** You'll be lively and confident with a pig spirit animal. You don't worry about what others think of you, and you aren't afraid to be goofy or embarrass yourself if that's what you want. You're a free spirit, and you live by your own rules rather than societies. You consider yourself lucky, and you are, and things just have a way of working out for you. Like your spirit animal, you're resourceful, and you can do anything you set your mind to. You're good with money, and you inspire others to succeed and become the best possible versions of themselves.

## 22. Elephant

Everybody loves elephants, and they're some of the most loving and kindest animals out there. They carry great symbolism as spirit animals and guides. In fact, elephants were viewed as symbols of great power and wisdom across many ancient civilizations and cultures, and they were revered. They represent endurance, maternal instincts, and a powerful connection to mother earth. Elephants act as a reminder to take care of ourselves and that we should have confidence in our own abilities because we can accomplish anything we want.

**As a Guide**: The elephant guide will help you stop and consider your needs before trying to help others. They often manifest before kind people who always put others' needs before their own to remind them that nothing is more important than nurturing one's self. It will guide you into finding the parts of yourself that need fulfillment and show you the path to fulfilling those needs, whether it's a professional goal or reconnecting with a family member. Elephants also symbolize protection and strength, and they will help you recognize your own strengths and power. With this, you can protect not only yourself and your loved ones but also your hopes and dreams.

**As a Spirit Animal:** Those with elephant spirit animals are often extremely intelligent, and their career paths show as much, excelling as scientists and scholars. They're strong-willed and tenacious, and they cannot be easily taken off course by blunders or roadblocks. They plow through obstacles with admirable resilience, and they have a great understanding of who they are as people. They value family and make for great parents, and they are very loyal to their own. Elephant people are also very compassionate, and they care for the helpless and the suffering of others. They have a lot of empathy that drives them to try to help those in need.

## 23. Frog

Frogs are another major symbol of transition and change. They're a constant reminder that nothing stays the same and that life is constantly changing and moving forward. Due to their aquatic nature, frogs are associated with cleansing in both a physical and spiritual sense. They are also associated with feminine energies and powerful emotions. When it enters your life, it is a sign that you need to find an opportunity in whatever transition you're going through. Frogs also symbolize creative powers that often accompany transformations and represent abundance and wealth.

**As a Guide:** The frog will leap into your life as you undergo a major transition for which you weren't necessarily ready. It will guide you through this difficult time and inspire you to find the silver lining in that transition. Frogs have often been associated with rebirth, and this spirit guide will help you view the change you're undergoing as a rebirth you can come out of like a new person with a different purpose. As it symbolizes cleansing, the frog will also help you get rid of negative energy in your life and surround yourself with only positive influences. It will show you how to better take care of yourself by shedding fears and negativity.

**As a Spirit Animal:** When you find out that your spirit animal is a frog, you'll find that you have many qualities shared by others around the world with the same spirit animal. You're a great listener, and people come to you for advice because you can relate to others easily and empathize with their pain. Your empathy is genuine, and you care about others and wish for them to feel better. You're a healer, and people who come in contact with you are all the better for it. You value home and family a great deal, and they play an important part in your life, no matter how far you go.

### 24. Panda

As silly and goofy as they may appear, pandas are actually very powerful spirit animals that inspire strength and willpower. Pandas help us remain grounded and represent a strong connection to the earth. Pandas also represent kindness and gentleness, especially when it comes to dealing with others. Pandas symbolize the unity between contrasting aspects of your personality, such as the masculine and feminine parts.

**As a Guide**: A panda as a spirit guide will remind you that gratitude is healthy for the mind, body, and soul. It will help you find that gratitude within yourself, so you can focus on giving others and helping people experience what you're experiencing. The panda will guide you into finding balance and leaning toward the positive things in your life rather than dwelling on the bad. Pandas often symbolize heightened awareness of surroundings, so a panda guide in your life can also help you become aware of things that aren't working for you and are causing you to be stressed out or frustrated so you can change them.

**As a Spirit Animal**: People with pandas as spirit animals are sensitive and can be very emotional. They often express this by needing physical and emotional comfort, but they are still independent and strong enough to go on without it. They're gentle and love being around others, but they equally enjoy solitude and even thrive in it. They're wise and smart, and they actively avoid meaningless conflict, but when they do get involved, they end it with their wisdom and ability to see through others.

## 25. Parrot

In many cases, parrots symbolize the importance of staying alert and mindful of new opportunities so that we may seize them. It's a constant reminder that anything is possible if you're prepared and alert. In some cultures, parrots represent the notion of learning new languages and developing that side of yourself. It could also mean that you need to be more positive with your self-talk and use more affirmations rather than criticism that doesn't help you in any way.

**As a Guide**: Parrot spirit guides will come into your life to give you a nudge in the right direction so you can go after your dreams, especially those you never thought possible. It will help you understand the importance of taking some time to listen to your inner voice and figure out what you really want out of life.

**As a Spirit Animal**: Those with parrots as spirit animals are very good with words and naturally eloquent. They are often diplomats or work in positions where the gift of talking is needed. They are very understanding and make for excellent listeners. They know when to talk and when to be quiet and listen, making them quite loved among their peers.

## 26. Rabbit

Rabbits represent several things in different contexts. They can be the fear that we have in the face of the unknown since rabbits tend to be timid. Yet, they are also very creative and represent fertility, love, and harmony. Many ancient cultures viewed rabbits as lucky charms and a symbol of abundance and prosperity. Despite their fearful nature, rabbits are quite gentle and kind, and they have a passion for life, which can be represented in their manifestations as spirit animals and guides.

**As a Guide**: The rabbit spirit guide will remind you of how creative you are and the vast resources you have, *which you may have* *forgotten about.* It will help you put those resources to good use and leverage them to push your life forward and pursue your dreams. This guide will also guide you to further plan for your future so you can reap the rewards of your hard work. A rabbit spirit guide might be the sign you need from the universe that you should have kids if this was something you were reluctant about. It will show you that you're ready and should move forward.

**As a Spirit Animal**: If the rabbit is your spirit animal, you're shy, and you may suffer from anxiety, but you don't let it cripple you, and you live your life with a sense of wonder and spontaneity. You're quick on your feet, and you don't get stuck easily. You're the observational type, and you're also very gentle. Despite your intelligence and wit, you don't use it to hurt others, and you don't use your intellect to show off. You're also creative, and you have the ability to solve problems that might stump others, which is why you're successful and very good at whatever you decide to do.

## 27. Scorpion

Scorpions are symbols of strength and the power that we all have within us and most often don't fully understand. It's also a reminder that you can use this power to delve into the unknown in search of success and fulfillment. It's a powerful ally and totem that can inspire confidence and courage in the face of adversity. It's also associated with observational powers and the importance of assessing your surroundings to understand what works for you and what doesn't.

**As a Guide**: Scorpions are powerful spirit guides that will help you in several ways. A scorpion will appear in your life when you need to evaluate your surroundings and the people/things around you. They will guide you through cutting off that which no longer serves you, from clutter around your home to toxic friends. It will help you shed your fear of failure and embrace your weaknesses so that you can turn them into strengths.

**As a Spirit Animal**: Scorpion people are strong both in will and demeanor. They're goal-oriented, and they have a great focus that they use to move ahead in life. They're also influential and can inspire and lead people. They're passionate and make great lovers, but they also enjoy solitary time between bouts of passion and affection. They're physical beings who care deeply for the sense of touch. True to the scorpion's symbolism representing new beginnings, those who have it as their spirit animal embrace change and can handle it with grace.

## 28. Turtle

Turtles show us that all we need is consistency and doing more of the same things to make it in life. They symbolize determination and serenity, as well as walking your path with humility and peacefulness, confident in knowing that you will make it. Moreover, turtles teach us that moving slow and steady is an opportunity to stop and enjoy the moment and admire our surroundings in all their beauty. We can learn a lot from observing turtles, who, as spirit animals, show us that you don't need to go big or be faster than your peers to accomplish your goals.

**As a Guide**: The turtle spirit guide will appear in your life when you are feeling distracted and all over the place. It will help ground you and steer you in the right direction so you can find your purpose once again. Turtles have also been associated with earth for a long time, so when this guide appears to you, it may be a sign that you need to spend some time in nature to ground yourself and find some peace. This spirit guide will help you focus on your goals and find serenity within yourself, which will happen when you slow down and pace yourself.

**As a Spirit Animal:** People with turtle spirit animals are peaceful, calm, and grounded. They are wise, and they think things through before they act. They don't let their emotions rule them. They are in tune with their emotions, just like the turtle is in tune with the earth, which helps them avoid overreacting. They're accepting of other people because they can always relate and see where others are coming from. They are also creative and focused, and that, paired with their relaxed and stress-free attitude, helps them achieve success and reach their goals.

## 29. Raccoon

Raccoons are some of the most adaptive animals out there, blessed with cleverness and the ability to solve problems. They teach us to take the time to assess a situation before trying to come up with an answer so we can succeed. They also show us how to look at the bigger picture rather than focusing on just our immediate needs. When a raccoon enters your life, it is most likely a sign that you need to be more accepting and grateful for the gifts you already have.

**As a Guide**: Raccoon spirit guides can enter your life when you're struggling to let go of something troubling you, whether that is a situation or a person, or even a belief. It will guide you to make peace with whatever is ailing you so you can move forward. It will also help you adapt to new realities that you might be struggling with, just like the raccoon's mask symbolizes our ability to shape-shift to adapt and grow rather than just mourning the past and what we lost.

**As a Spirit Animal**: You know all sides of your personality, and you are in tune with your feelings and thoughts. You easily adapt to change and move on from pain faster than others around you. You're also charming, and people often find you charismatic, so people like to spend time around you. A curious part of you drives you into exploring new things and constantly trying to satisfy your hunger for learning and experience. You don't like to be still and prefer to try new activities. People see you, and they see more than charm; they also see intellect and creativity, which helps you move forward in the professional world.

## 30. Penguin

A lot of noble qualities are associated with penguins, like confidence, sacrifice, and determination. These wobbly creatures remind us that there is a certain order and pattern to the chaos that surrounds us. There is hope if you persist, and as long as you keep trying, you will get there. Penguins inspire confidence in the advent of good things even right after so much bad has happened.

**As a Guide:** Penguin is another spirit guide that can help you find balance in your life, known for its adaptive qualities. It will show you how you can remain flexible and balanced, even in the face of chaos and adversity. Penguin guides can help you remain centered and focused on the bigger picture so you can continue to work toward your goals. They also symbolize a strong connection between physical and spiritual planes, and they will show you that connection and help you leverage it in life.

**As a Spirit Animal:** Penguin people are highly capable; they're creators who make things and get the job done better than anyone. They adapt to any situation, and they ace new jobs quickly. They know where they're going and what they want out of life, and they're excellent team players. They have a superior connection to the spiritual realm, and they walk the line between it and the physical realm with ease, which is why many of them have a knack for lucid dreaming.

## 31. Dog

Everyone loves dogs, and they are truly man's best friend, but dogs also carry a powerful spiritual symbolism. Dogs' loyalty is perhaps their greatest attribute, and as spirit animals, this plays a significant role in how we perceive them as well as ourselves. Dogs also represent courage and devotion, not to mention protection and patience. They are companions and partners, and humans stand to learn much from dogs. Despite their domestication over the past few centuries, dogs have retained many of their qualities, especially the instinct to protect loved ones and value their pack.

**As a Guide**: A dog spirit guide will appear in your life if you have experienced betrayal or powerful feelings of loneliness. They will remind you that there is loyalty out there and that you're not alone. It will help you find kindness within you and inspire you to use it as a tool rather than indulging in criticism and harshness. Dog spirit guides help their humans be better to others and spread love and kindness. It will also help you accept your path and embrace the journey rather than dwelling on what might have been. Perhaps the most important way a dog spirit guide will help you is to remind you that nothing is more important than being loyal and truthful to yourself.

**As a Spirit Guide:** If your spirit animal is a dog, you're honest and have a large capacity for love. Your spirit is unwavering, and you wear your heart on your sleeve. You're naturally loyal to the point of giving your life to protect the ones you love if needed. You don't have it in you to be deceptive or treacherous, and you're an excellent judge of character. Your kindness drives you to spend a lot of time and effort to help others because of your natural instincts to protect and help those in need. Your empathy and trustworthiness know no limitations, and a dog as your spirit animal always feeds that part of you and enhances those qualities in your personality.

## 32. Fox

Foxes get a bad reputation as deceivers and tricksters, but they are, in fact, powerful spirit animals, and they can teach us much. They are symbols of creativity, adaptability, and wisdom, and many civilizations viewed them as good luck totems. They can teach us how to adapt to new situations and find a way around obstacles. Their wisdom is inspiring and can help us think quickly on our feet and find answers to difficult problems.

**As a Guide**: A fox spirit guide will appear before you when you're stuck with a challenge. It will remind you that the answer is right before you. It will help you remain centered and focused until you can find a way around the problem. The fox guide will bless you with patience and persistence so you can keep working at it until you finally get where you want to. A fox spirit guide can appear before you as a sign that you need to sharpen up, whether mentally or physically. The fox may also be trying to alert you of impending deception from someone in your life or that someone is trying to hurt you from the shadows. It will help you open your eyes and see the reality of your situation.

**As a Spirit Animal**: Those with fox spirit animals are also very loyal, and they would do anything in their power to protect their loved ones. They're full of energy and life, and people love to be around them for that reason. They know how to fit in any group using their wits and cleverness. They are careful observers, and they have a great eye for detail, which helps them blend in easily and see through people's motives. They don't tackle obstacles head-on but rather find a clever way around them.

## 33. Swan

Swans are beautiful creatures that have a powerful spiritual symbolism. A swan represents acceptance and going with the flow rather than lingering on pain and frustration. It can teach us to trust our instincts and intuition, especially when it comes to the future. It will remind us to listen to the feminine aspects of our personality too. They symbolize beauty and grace, and they remind us that we can always see a challenge from a different perspective, which might just be what we need.

**As a Guide:** A swan spirit guide will present itself at a time when you're feeling stagnant. It will guide you through developing your intuition and accessing an altered state of awareness. You can then use this to turn your life around. She will show you a new path and how you can walk it, but she'll also teach you how to be more accepting of your fate and embrace the gifts you've been given. The swan guide will help you trust your instincts and your vision of the future to move forward, knowing that this is the right path for you.

**As a Spiritual Animal:** People with a swan as a spirit animal embody many of its majestic qualities. There's an air of grace to them, and they are beautiful people inside and out. They carry themselves with pride and elegance, and others respect them deeply for it. They're also very devoted, and they are often content with their lives. Swan people have a great ability to heal, and they're constantly changing and transforming. They believe in true love, and they are very loyal once they find their significant other. They are also great at balancing the personal and professional aspects of their lives.

## 34. Giraffe

Individuality has often been one of the defining characteristics associated with the giraffe, which also applies to the spirit animal. Giraffes are kind, and their tall necks make them a powerful and revered spirit animal with significant symbolism. They can teach us to follow our foresight and trust our feelings so we can walk down the path of success confidently and without fear. Moreover, another way to consider giraffes' symbolism is that they remind us that it's okay to ask for help and seek guidance from others because there's no shame in it.

**As a Guide:** A giraffe spirit guide will appear to help you listen to your inner voice and follow it down the path of success. It will show you how to listen to your heart and trust that you know what's best for you, which many people struggle with. The giraffe guide will center you and help you find peace in your life. It's there, you just need to find it, and this spirit guide will help you find and embrace it. You will find calm and serenity where you never thought possible, and you'll be able to move forward in your life with a little less pain and anxiety.

**As a Spirit Animal**: Giraffe people are kind, gentle, peaceful beings who like to meditate and value their serenity and time of tranquility. They take their time when they're doing things, and they see no value in getting to the finish line first. They do things their way, unfazed by a peer or societal pressure, which is often why they're happier and more grounded than their peers. They have higher perceptions, and their inner awareness is unrivaled. When they make a mistake, they can look inward with ease and find out why they made that mistake and how they can avoid it in the future, and they do it without flogging themselves and being overly critical. Their perception and vision of the future are often true, which is why they almost always succeed in achieving the goals they had set for themselves.

## 35. Firefly

Fireflies represent the light that we all carry inside. It's also a reminder that it is good in people; we just need to look for it rather than just focusing on the bad in others. Fireflies teach us that it's not the appearance that counts but rather what's on the inside. They convey a very important message of simplicity. Things don't have to be complicated, but it's us that often complicate them. Fireflies remind us that we need to define ourselves by our good qualities, not our faults and shortcomings.

**As a Guide:** Fireflies will come to you as a spirit guide when you're feeling frustrated to remind you of the past. Fireflies represent the childhood wonders and the beauty and magic in all things. They will enter your life as guides to restore that awe and help you rekindle your passion for life and the excitement for all things new. They will guide you down that path of innocence and purity and simplicity, which you'll walk to find that passion you had long lost due to monotony and routine.

**As a Spirit Animal**: Those lucky enough to have fireflies as their spirit animal are free spirits, wanderers who don't shy away from any new experience. They live their lives with passion and spontaneity, and they make their own choices without influence from others. They're creative and hardworking, and it would take a lot to snuff that spark within that keeps them going. Firefly people inspire others, and people feel alive around them, and the light they carry shines on through their actions and words.

## 36. Mosquito

We might hate them, and we often say that mosquitos have no inherent value or meaning in life besides causing pain, but this isn't exactly true. Mosquitos actually carry universal wisdom, and their symbolism lies in how they represent self-worth. A mosquito reminds us to look after our emotional and mental wellbeing because nothing matters more. Mosquitos are also associated with feminine attributes and assertiveness, and self-sacrifice is another characteristic associated with mosquitos.

**As a Guide:** Mosquito as a spirit guide will show you that your ambition matters and you have what it takes to make it. No dream is impossible as long as you work hard enough. Mosquito guides can also show you how to make new discoveries about yourself and your abilities so that you can move forward in life. It will also help you maintain positive energy and keep negative people out of your life. The mosquito will show you how to utilize your time and take advantage of your opportunities. Moreover, mosquitos signify the importance of having a plan and sticking to it until you get what you want.

**As a Spirit Animal**: If you have a mosquito as your spirit animal, you're creative and smart. Despite the situation, you can also adapt very easily to wherever you are. You're ambitious and enjoy being successful, but you also understand that success isn't the only thing that matters in life. You care a lot about the people in your life, and you're willing to make great sacrifices to make them happy. You're a proud person, and you have high regard for yourself, so you don't let others abuse you. Your reputation precedes you like someone to admire but never mess with.

## 37. Raven

Ravens are mystical and magical creatures with major spiritual symbolism. Some believe that a raven in your life means that magic is involved, whether you know it or not. A raven may enter your life to remind you to listen to the messages the universe is trying to tell you and heed your spirit guides' warnings. Ravens are messengers, so their presence often means that there is a message to be delivered; we just need to listen carefully. Ravens often signify an impending change you should be prepared for, so keep that in mind.

**As a Guide:** Ravens are keepers of synchronicity, and they can bend time and space, so as a spirit guide, the raven can help you find comfort in knowing that you are in the right place and the right time. You are where you need to be in life, and renewal and rebirth are afoot. They can help you through any major transition and guide you through challenging times where you need to heal. Ravens can guide you on your journey and help you with clues and insight so you can work on your goals, and like crows, ravens are heralds of magic. So, keep an eye out for any magical occurrences in your life.

**As a Spirit Guide:** Those with the raven as their spirit guide have the gift of insight; in challenging or tricky situations, they can see things others cannot. They have heightened awareness and sometimes even psychic abilities. They are creative and playful, but they also enjoy some quiet time and their own company. Raven people are wise, and they strongly connect to the spirit world. They often act as a bridge between the spiritual and physical realms, receiving and delivering messages to and from those realms.

### 38. Panther

Panthers represent courage, power, agility, and aggression. They are fiercely protective of their loved ones. Panthers symbolize feminine powers, too, and have often been associated with the Mother and the power of the night (moon phases as well). The symbolism of the panther also varies depending on its color. For instance, black panthers represent the notion that there is hope and light at the end of a dark tunnel, meaning you can get out of your slump and bounce back from tragedy.

**As a Guide**: A panther guide appearing in your life indicates that it's time for you to discover your deepest desires and start a new chapter in your life. It will help you live your dreams and expand your awareness. The panther guide will accompany you on this journey of self-discovery and act as your personal guide. The panther's raw power will help you wade through the darkness and unlock your potential.

**As a Spirit Animal**: If your spirit animal is a panther, you're an exotic person, and you have a wild spirit. You are graceful, and you carry yourself with pride. You're also powerful, and people don't want to make an enemy out of you. While you are loyal to and protective of your loved ones, you're also a loner, and you enjoy spending time on your own.

### 39. Rat

Rats are arguably the most hated rodents, but they are also symbols of fertility, strength, tenacity, and intelligence. Rats come into people's lives to remind them to assert themselves and explore new horizons. It could be a new hobby or something you've always wanted to try, and with the coming of the rat, you should.

**As a Guide:** The rat spirit guide will come into your life when you're ready to try something new and turn a new page. It will help you get rid of uncertainty and doubt as you make your first steps toward a new beginning. The rat guide might also notify you of the importance of clearing any clutter in your life and doing a cleansing, which can relate to emotional or physical baggage.

**As a Spirit Animal**: Those who have rats as their spirit animal are some of the most relentless you can ever meet. They never stop until they achieve their goals, and they are always searching for new ways to get ahead in life. They're successful and smart when it comes to business. They are also very adaptive, and they can survive transitions and changes and come out on top.

# Conclusion

After reading this book, you now have extensive knowledge about Animism in Shamanism. Ancient peoples have always recognized the role of animals, the power that Animal Spirit Guides hold, as well as the importance of forming harmonious relationships with them.

This book offered a great deal of insight into Shamanic traditions, especially when it comes to animals and acknowledging their unique energies and spirits. Shamans and healers know how incredible calling upon an animal can be to seek its guidance and support. Understanding that Animal Spirit Guides can provide us with the needed protection, guidance, and support that we need to make the best out of our life journey allows us to thrive. This book showed you these creatures' role as our teachers, allies, and guides. It helped you better understand the amount of power, strength, and courage these guides can bring into our lives.

Implementing this book's invaluable knowledge can help you transform your life. Not only will you be highly aware of all the lessons you need to learn, as well as acquire all the strength, courage, and skills you need to overcome any challenges or obstacles that come your way, but you will also feel more in tune and aligned with your mind, body, and spirit. Connecting with your Spirit, Power, and Totem Animal does not only help you stay out of trouble to make your life easier, but it also helps you become more grounded and self-aware. Bonding with our guide teaches us humility and respect, and it teaches us about our duties and responsibilities toward life, ourselves, and the surrounding nature.

These creatures can give you an indispensable understanding of how you can use your powers. They are proof that the ability to change lies within you. You don't need to adopt an alternate behavior or personality. Being open to opportunity, learning, evolving, and channeling your skills and power in the right places is all you need to do to emerge successfully from your journey —*exactly* what your Animal Spirit Guide and Power Animal are here to do.

While any real change comes from within, this book serves as a guide on finding your personal guides, feeling their presence, and identifying the lessons they're here to teach you. Reading this book will make you more receptive to the information, experiences, and wisdom that these creatures are here to share with you. You have all the knowledge to trustingly, confidently, and peacefully give into your Spirit Animal's support. You are now open to feeling its presence and connecting with it on a deeper level. Understanding and embracing their energies and medicines can help clarify their messages.

Forming a bond with your Power Animal can help you learn more about your true self than you ever thought possible. You will get to understand your authentic self in ways you never did before. This healing journey can help you rediscover your life's purpose, overcome any obstacle or challenges, and bring meaning to your life.

Made in the USA
Columbia, SC
01 May 2024

35158676R00063